ANALYSES

Africa's future ...
can biosciences
contribute?

**Analyses: Africa's future ...
can biosciences contribute?**

Essays compiled by Patrick Mitton and David Bennett, St Edmund's College, Cambridge CB3 0BN

Published in 2015 by Banson, 27 Devonshire Road, Cambridge CB1 2BH

ISBN 978-0-9932932-3-8

Citation: Mitton, P. and Bennett, D. (eds.) 2015. *Analyses: Africa's Future ... Can Biosciences Contribute?* Banson/B4FA.

This project was made possible through the support of grants from the John Templeton Foundation, the Malaysian Commonwealth Studies Centre and the Cambridge Malaysian Education and Development Trust.

The opinions expressed in this publication are those of the authors and do not necessarily reflect the views of the John Templeton Foundation, the Malaysian Commonwealth Studies Centre, the Cambridge Malaysian Education and Development Trust, B4FA or Banson.

Design and layout: Banson

Printed in the UK by Lavenham Press

ANALYSES

Africa's future ...
can biosciences
contribute?

Productivity growth in small family farms contributes to more inclusive growth, not only by reducing the prices of staple foods but also by improving access to food.

The State of Food Insecurity in the World 2015, Food and Agriculture Organization of the United Nations (FAO)

Biotechnology represents a powerful tool that augments conventional approaches to tackling the future challenge of food security.

Professor Walter S. Alhassan, Forum for Agriculture Research in Africa (FARA)

In 30 years we'll have a population of 9 billion people to feed and that will increase demand for the quantity and diversity of the food that we need. That's why we have to consider genetic modification as one of the tools – but not the only tool – that would help humanity to address those challenges.

Calestous Juma, Professor of the Practice of International Development, Harvard Kennedy School

In a world of plenty, no one, not a single person, should go hungry. But almost a billion still do not have enough to eat. I want to see an end to hunger everywhere within my lifetime.

Ban Ki-moon, United Nations Secretary-General

The economies of many African countries are growing faster than anywhere else in the world – and agriculture, which accounts for a third of Africa's GDP, is poised to be the next installment of the "Africa rising" narrative.

Dr Agnes Kalibata, President, Alliance for the Green Revolution in Africa (AGRA)

Africa is home to about 60 per cent of all available uncultivated agricultural land. But that is Africa's strategic reserve … we have to increase productivity of existing farming systems. We have to become modern … the potential is there.

Kanayo Nwanze, President, International Fund for Agricultural Development (IFAD)

5

Foreword

Forecasts for the inextricably linked scourges of food insecurity and poverty are bleakly familiar. According to the United Nations, "over the next fifteen years, the world population is expected to increase by 1.1 billion so that by 2030, the global economy will need to support approximately 8.4 billion people ... Africa will account for more than 40 per cent of the global increase in population". With qualified positivism, in 2015 the Food and Agriculture Organization of the United Nations (FAO) reported that "the number of hungry people in the world has dropped to 795 million ... or around one person out of every nine". Meanwhile, as the World Bank reported, "17 per cent of people in the developing world lived at or below $1.25 a day". Crucially, as the International Fund for Agricultural Development estimates, "there are about 500 million small farms in developing countries, supporting almost 2 billion people". And these are the people largely involved in those grim statistics. Yet some African countries are now among the world's fastest growing economies with huge natural resources – the African Development Bank forecasts that the continent's gross domestic product (GDP) growth rate will strengthen to 5 per cent in 2016. But Africa is still unfortunately lacking in skills, infrastructure and governance. A vast range of issues must be faced if the challenges of food security are to be met.

It was in this context that the John Templeton Foundation, an independent philanthropic organisation, funded the programme Biosciences for Farming in Africa (http://b4fa.org), concentrating on crop production by smallholder farmers. Associated with this programme, the Foundation funded selected projects aimed at investigating the best practices and policies for implementing genetic modification (GM) and other recent advances in genetic technologies in the local crops grown by these farmers. These projects have been carried out by some of the world's leading researchers and their groups from the USA, UK and Africa.

This book summarises many of the key findings and recommendations of 13 of the funded projects in essays intended for readers looking for the principal messages emanating from the research work of each project. The book will be of interest to policy makers and their advisers, educationalists, members of non-governmental organisations and the media, as well as those who take an interest in smallholder agriculture. For those seeking an in-depth analysis of the project outcomes, scientific articles published elsewhere give further detail. Many of the authors have referenced some of the scientific journals that have published such works.

Questions outlined in this book include: what are the scientifically established nutritional, social, environmental and regulatory consequences of crops generated by genetic modification together with other modern genetic techniques, particularly for small landholders; can the use of these crops have economic impacts in less-developed countries; and what are the barriers to acceptance and use of these crops?

The crops represented in this book are those commonly grown by smallholder farmers for staple foods, including maize, cassava, cooking banana, sorghum and rice. The primary focus is Sub-Saharan Africa, but some chapters offer experience from around the world, including China, India, the Philippines and Honduras. All sections of the supply chain are represented by the projects, from plant genetics, regulatory status, seed supply and agronomy extension services, through to grower and societal perception. Many in-depth interviews and focus group discussions were conducted to ascertain first-hand knowledge and an understanding of the crop production techniques used by growers and stakeholders in the various countries studied.

These essays, summarising the results of wide-ranging expert research, are intended to provide interesting and informative reading, and, in doing so, contribute to balanced, informed and broad discussions as well as political, community and personal decisions.

The book aims to contribute positively to the debate on modern advances in plant genetics and thereby play a small part in alleviating the food insecurity and poverty of many hundreds of millions of people around the world.

Patrick J. Mitton and David J. Bennett
St Edmund's College, Cambridge, UK

Contents

Foreword   6

1. **The GM debate in East Africa**   11
   Kristin Wedding and Johanna Nesseth
2. **Global lessons for agricultural sustainability from GM crops**   21
   Phil Macnaghten and Susana Carro-Ripalda
3. **Can GM crops help African farmers? Insights from Uganda**   28
   Matthew A. Schnurr, Lincoln Addison, Sarah Mujabi-Mujuzi
   and Tonny Miiro
4. **Adoption of GM crops in Africa: why the seed sector matters**   36
   Edward Mabaya
5. **Using a Community of Practice to learn from smallholders in**   46
   South Africa
   Mary K. Hendrickson, Jere L. Gilles, William H. Meyers,
   Kenneth C. Schneeberger and William R. Folk
6. **Biotechnology regulatory systems: implications for food**   54
   security and rural livelihoods
   Samuel E. Timpo, Diran Makinde, Godwin N.Y. Lemgo,
   Hashini G. Dissanayake, Joseph Guenthner and Karim Maredia
7. **Assessing and communicating the risks and benefits of GM**   62
   cassava in Kenya
   Harvey James, Corinne Valdivia, William R. Folk, Dekha Sheikh,
   Festus Murithi, Violet Gathaara, Milton Kengo, Charles Bett
   and Grace Mbure

Analyses

8. Disease-resistant GM cassava in Uganda and Kenya during a pandemic 76
Nigel J. Taylor, Haruna A. Sekabira, Kenneth W. Sibiko, Anton Bua and John Lynam

9. The politics and economics of GM food production in China, India and Kenya 86
Carl E. Pray, Jikun Huang, Jun Yang, Ruifa Hu, Latha Nagarajan, Bharat Ramaswami, Anwar Naseem, Gal Hochman, and Sanjib Bhuyan

10. Adoption and uptake pathways of biotech crops for small-scale farmers in China, India and the Philippines 95
Mariechel J. Navarro and Randy A. Hautea

11. Honduras and *Bt*/HT maize – a small country model for GM crop adoption? 106
José Falck Zepeda, Patricia Zambrano, Denisse McLean, Arie Sanders, Maria Mercedes Roca, Cecilia Chi-Ham and Alan Bennett

12. Seeking sustainability for smallholders: *Bt* cotton in India 119
Glenn Davis Stone and Andrew Flachs

13. Identifying and analysing barriers to the acceptance and use of GM rice 129
Eric Wailes, Alvaro Durand-Morat, Eddie Chavez, Mohammad Alam, Francis Mwaijande, Hans De Steur, Shoichi Ito, Zhihao Zheng, Alice Jin (Jiang), Ranjit Mane and Francis Tsiboe

Index 138

The GM debate in East Africa

Kristin Wedding and Johanna Nesseth

The role genetically modified (GM) crops can play in meeting Africa's long-term food security needs is a serious debate. There are many challenges hampering African agricultural productivity and, given that only a third of African lands use even basic hybrid seed, countries and donors must carefully evaluate the benefit of investing in GM technology, especially if it comes at the expense of other parts of the agriculture sector.

During the course of a 12-month period, from 2012 through 2013, the Center for Strategic and International Studies (CSIS) undertook research to assess the potential for GM crops to contribute to food security in East Africa. Our three-person research team spent a week in each of three countries: Kenya, Tanzania and Uganda. We interviewed more than 150 people, and visited farms, research stations, media outlets and non-governmental organisations (NGOs). Our goal was to assess the state of the public debate and views of smallholder farmers, and gain a better understanding of the status of bio-technology research, regulatory and legislative efforts related to GM crops, and the forecast for adoption.

In many ways, the GM debates in Kenya, Tanzania and Uganda mirror global trends

In many ways, the GM debates in Kenya, Tanzania and Uganda mirror global trends. As the agriculture sector in each country continues to develop, so does the highly

Overall ... politicians and the public have not been effectively engaged with objective scientific evidence that articulates exactly what the technology is, how it works, and how it might address food security challenges

polarised debate, often reflecting the strife experienced in the USA and Europe. The absence of commercially available products and significant communication gaps between key stakeholders compounds the confusion. Overall, in the three focus countries, politicians and the public have not been effectively engaged with objective scientific evidence that articulates exactly what the technology is, how it works, and how it might address food security challenges. While some forums for open discussion and exchange exist, debates are often intense and emotional, making it challenging to determine the path that will best benefit the country. Ultimately, GM crop cultivation in any of the countries could have a significant impact in the region. The three countries watch each other closely, and their economies are closely linked. If any of the countries commercialises GM crops it will be difficult to contain these crops within national borders.

Compared to its neighbours, Kenya embarked on an early path towards cultivating and regulating GM crops. It has led the region in developing a robust regulatory system and building its scientific capacity. Kenya has established a regulatory agency for biotechnology review and approval, and the country's advanced scientific community has a number of confined field trials underway in GM cassava, maize, sorghum and cotton. But a legal framework alone does not ensure the development and commercialisation of these crops, especially when the regulatory system is subject to political whims. In November 2012, Kenya's Minister of Public Health and Sanitation convinced the cabinet to support her ban on GM food products. In effect, the Kenyan government disregarded its own biosafety experts and regulatory legal system, which is indicative of the role that politics and personalities will play in the development and commercialisation of GM products.

Kenya may be better positioned over the long run, but has not had the concentrated focus from government that is needed in the absence of concerted demand from farmers for new varieties of crops.

Tanzania has an uphill battle in adopting the technology, with great public antipathy towards GM crops and general mistrust of private companies seeking to make a profit at the expense of farmers and the environment. Tanzania's regulatory system is among the most restrictive and precautionary in Africa, and includes policies of strict liability and strict redress. The President has equivocated in his support of GM technology, and there is internal political opposition among some of the ministries. However, as the recipient of significant US and other foreign assistance in agriculture, the Tanzanian government is under pressure to develop a more accepting regulatory position towards GM crops, which would create a more inviting agricultural investment environment. Tanzania has a strong but comparatively small scientific community that is frustrated by the restrictions on advanced research. Like Kenya and Uganda, Tanzania is part of the Water Efficient Maize for Africa (WEMA) project, which in addition to developing conventional drought-tolerant varieties is research-ing GM varieties. However, Tanzania's regulatory structure has prevented it from conducting confined field trials

If Kenya, Tanzania or Uganda commercialises GM crops it will be difficult to contain these crops within national borders

13

Countries that do wish to pursue GM crops should be prepared for a long process that requires sustained effort from a host of different constituents

of the GM varieties as the government has deferred participation in the GM component of the project. Regardless of Tanzania's policies, should its neighbouring countries adopt GM crops, the porous borders would allow seeds to be easily transported into Tanzania – intentionally or not.

Uganda's burgeoning scientific capacity, research efforts and developing biosafety regulatory system have resulted in both regulatory and research progress. Uganda has worked to move legislation through parliament, emphasising the importance of biotechnology for reducing pests and diseases that impair food security. At the same time, research centres are advancing trials on bananas that have made headway but still have not achieved the variety that will fully appeal to the Ugandan palate. Although its barriers to adoption are lower than Kenya's and Tanzania's given its less open political environment, it acknowledges that there is still a long road ahead.

Though Uganda undertook GM research to combat diseases that were destroying bananas, the country's staple food crop, there is not yet a driving demand for GM products among end users – farmers and consumers.

Main observations
GM debate
It is widely recognised among the countries' scientific communities that GM crops could have a significant impact in addressing specific challenges, including improving productivity, combating crop diseases, enhancing the nutritional content of food, and mitigating impacts from climate change.

However, the nature of GM research and regulation is distinctly reflective of each country's local context and governance system. Opinions tend to follow the same trends as the global debate, in part due to the fact that both research initiatives and opposition groups are often funded by European and US NGOs and governments. Political will matters greatly for this issue. Because this is a niche topic among African policy makers and there is not a strong demand signal from farmers, a political champion is required to see the issue through the government and legislature. Leadership and political will significantly impact broader attitudes towards GM products, along with ongoing and future GM research, development, adoption and commercialisation.

Sustaining momentum on the development and regulation of GM crops will be difficult in the face of a variety of forces: vocal opposition from a small constituency of highly engaged activists, bureaucratic inertia or ambivalence, and long delays as products move through the testing procedure. Countries that do wish to pursue GM crops should be prepared for a long process that requires sustained effort from a host of different constituents.

Investment in agricultural delivery systems is essential

Even in the event of successful commercialisation, poor agricultural infrastructure and the lack of effective channels to disseminate technology to smallholder farmers is an overarching challenge. The large majority of smallholder farmers have not adopted basic existing technologies and practices. Extension systems remain chronically weak and could dampen any potential impact of GM crops should a country choose to adopt them. New and

The seed sector in each country is weak, cannot meet current demand and is often infiltrated with counterfeit products

15

To increase demand, products with desirable traits need to be on the market and available for farmers to choose

creative approaches to extension and education in agriculture must become a priority.

The seed sector in each country is weak and unable to meet current demand, and is often infiltrated with counterfeit products. Estimates from domestic trade organisations note that less than a third of farmers in Sub-Saharan Africa plant improved seed varieties, and representatives stated that seed breeders and distributors are unable to meet demand. For GM crops to make an impact in the region, scientists, businesses, policy makers and other interested parties need to work on the supply side, focusing both on quantity and quality. To increase demand, products with desirable traits need to be on the market and available for farmers to choose. Currently, most of the products under development do not meet the taste, appearance or cooking preferences of most consumers – highlighting the inherent challenge of GM crops in a setting where farmers are the consumers, unlike in many developed countries where farmers do not routinely consume the GM crops they grow.

Regulatory capacity

It is clear that political bureaucracy plays a determining factor in the development of biosafety regulatory systems and the degree to which they foster the development of GM crops. The institutional structure that governs agricultural research, agricultural policy and biosafety plays an important role in advancing research and implementation. The particular focus of each regulatory system has an important bearing on the potential for development and adoption. In Uganda, the environment is enabling and communications are quite uniform. Governing structures around biosafety have been generally well harmonised, with an early and consistent consultative process within government and greater consensus on the balance to be struck between biotechnology promotion and biosafety precaution. In Kenya, the regulatory system is robust but potentially limiting and subject to political intervention. In Tanzania, it is highly restrictive and the divisions and lines of authority around biosafety issues have created occasional tensions and jurisdictional uncertainties.[1]

Scientific capacity

African researchers are adapting donated GM varieties – for sweet potatoes, cassava and other crops – for relevance and preference within their individual countries. They are keen to drive the development of relevant transgenic technologies within their respective countries and throughout the region. Within the scientific establishment in each country visited, there is a sense of pride in the local advances in biotechnology and an eagerness to harness science to solve national and regional food security and development challenges. In each country, GM technologies will be developed and owned by public research facilities, so concerns about intellectual property rights are largely irrelevant even though these concerns still persist among many NGOs and with the general public. Many within the research establishment say that they need to better educate the public and policy makers on GM products and more effectively communicate the benefits and possible risks.

African researchers are keen to drive the development of relevant transgenic technologies within their respective countries and throughout the region

Smallholder farmers

There has been little systematic study of smallholder attitudes towards genetic

Scientific progress will be enhanced if researchers have the opportunity to push their research and findings into new areas of discovery

modification and, because GM crops have not yet become publicly available, their potential remains a largely abstract concept. One view, expressed by a senior official at the Ugandan Science Foundation for Livelihoods and Development, is that "farmers are open to options as long as they work, and as long as it gives some value added".[2]

But without a product available to make that calculation, there is no strong demand signal from smallholder farmers for the technologies, and other pressing priorities at present take precedence.

Farmers will need good products and information in order to shift to using GM crops. Subscription-based services, enhanced extension efforts and community-based farm leaders may be able to perform the role of trainers and educators.

Regional and trade dynamics

There is a fear that the commercialisation of GM food crops by East African Community (EAC) countries could negatively impact export markets. However, when analysing trade data for GM crops under development (maize, cotton and cassava) there is little evidence that commercialisation would pose significant trade losses, as the majority of these crops are staple food products traded intra-regionally not internationally.

Work is being conducted by a small group of experts through regional bodies such as the EAC and Common Market for East and Southern Africa (COMESA), but national policies and decisions will likely shape regional regulation of GM products. Nonetheless, as Uganda and Kenya move towards possible commercialisation of GM crops, the EAC will need a more harmonised framework for export, trade and biosafety regulation within member countries. Successful commercialisation of GM crops by one of these countries could accelerate adoption in the region as farmers and policy makers gain more tangible evidence of the possible benefits and drawbacks.

Conclusion

In the course of our research effort it became clear that there are two important reasons why governments and donors have chosen to focus on genetic engineering and biotechnology. One is that they have the potential to play an important role in battling pernicious pests and diseases as well as improving nutrition and reducing the use of water and chemicals, all of which can benefit farmers and consumers. Secondly, scientific progress will be enhanced if researchers have the opportunity to push their research and findings into new areas of discovery. There are scientific communities and research facilities in each country to host this activity, and there are scientists in developed-country universities and companies that are partners on the research efforts. However, each country has to overcome significant hurdles to the development and adoption of the technology.

As Kenya, Tanzania and Uganda move forward in their domestic debates on GM crops, it will be important for their governments, donors, the media and scientists to prioritise pathways for agricultural research that will have the greatest impact on food

It will be important for governments, donors, the media and scientists to prioritise pathways for agricultural research

19

security in East Africa. GM crops may very well play an important role but, in all cases, for any technology to truly contribute to development and food security, the broader agricultural systems will require sustained and focused investments. Such investments would enable scientists to produce research and outcomes that will promote food security in their countries, improve extension and education for farmers to learn and adopt new methods of planting and stewardship, and build reliable seed systems with the capacity to meet demand with legitimate products.

References
1. **Chambers, J. (2013).** *Biosafety of GM Crops in Kenya, Tanzania, and Uganda.* Rowman and Littlefield, Lanham, MD, USA.
2. **Arthur Makara.** Personal communication.

Authors
Kristin Wedding, Deputy Director and Fellow, Global Food Security Project, Center For Strategic and International Studies, Washington, DC, USA
Johanna Nesseth, Senior Vice President, Strategic Planning, Center For Strategic and International Studies, Washington, DC, USA

Global lessons for agricultural sustainability from GM crops

Phil Macnaghten and Susana Carro-Ripalda

With rising world populations, persistent hunger and chronic, growing demand for food globally, the need to protect land for biodiversity and ecosystem services, and the mounting threats associated with climate change, it is unsurprising that advances in the biosciences – and in the development of genetically modified (GM) crops in particular – are proposed to play a critical role in meeting the challenges of global food security.

Yet, although the rise of GM crops has been dramatic, their uptake has not been the smooth nor universal transition predicted by its advocates. Controversy has been marked, even in those countries where approvals have been impressively rapid. All too commonly, the regulation of GM crops has been challenged as inadequate, even biased – and in some settings, such as India and Mexico, the planting of certain crops has been judicially suspended.

The strategic question for this John Templeton Foundation project, led by Durham University and with international partners in Mexico, Brazil and India, was to examine why GM crops have not been universally accepted as a public good, since if we do not address this we will fail to understand the conditions under which GM crops may contribute to global food security in an inclusive manner.

All too commonly, the regulation of GM crops has been challenged as inadequate, even biased

21

The public debate surrounding GM crops has been reduced to one of safety

Current approaches to the regulation and governance of GM crops have been dominated by risk-based assessment methodologies, the assumption being that the key criterion mediating the release of GM products into the environment should be an independent case-by-case risk assessment of their impact on human health and the environment. One consequence is that the public debate surrounding GM crops has been reduced to one of safety: whether they are safe to eat and whether they are safe for the environment. In relation to these questions we remain agnostic. Our argument is otherwise. Our argument is that if we are to govern GM crops in a socially and scientifically robust fashion, we need to engage with the issue within the terms of the debate as it is considered by an inclusive array of actors.

At the core of the project was fieldwork undertaken in three of the global rising powers, namely Mexico (on GM maize), Brazil (on GM soya) and India (on GM cotton), and involving ethnographic, interview and focus group research with farmers, scientists and the public.[1, 2] The choice of three rising-power Global South case studies is deliberate. Most of the scholarship on GM crops has focused on Global North settings with – to date – relatively minor engagement with the dynamics of the issue in the Global South. Yet it will be in countries such as Brazil, Mexico and India, where agricultural innovation is most needed, that the bulk of food provision is expected to take place and where debates over GM agricultural technologies are likely to be most intense.

In Mexico, we found that the public debate on GM maize has been deeply controversial and culturally resonant, that protests against GM maize were widespread, and that they signified the defence of Mexican culture and identity in the face of unwanted forms of globalisation. We saw that decisions by regulatory bodies had been compromised and lacked transparency, and that there has been little sustained effort by involved institutions, including the Mexican state, to engage with the public. In our ethnographic field research, we found that farmers retain strong and enduring relations around maize agriculture and that the prospect of GM maize is seen as an intrusion on traditional practices. In our ethnographic research with scientists, we found a clear distinction within the laboratory between senior and older researchers who were more avowedly in favour of the application of GM agricultural technologies, and younger and more junior researchers who were more cautious and nuanced. Meanwhile, in our research with the urban public, we found a generally negative reaction to GM crops and foods, reflecting deep-seated mistrust in the Mexican government and its apparent collusion with large business corporations.

In Brazil, we found that even though the coverage of GM crops had risen rapidly since 2005 (mostly GM soya and maize), the issue was far from settled, with little evidence of public acceptance or inclusive governance. In our ethnographic field research, we found evidence of a conflict between the farmers and the technical experts from seed companies, each blaming the other for the growing problem of weed resistance to glyphosate. In our ethnographic research with scientists, we found clear and un-qualified optimism amongst scientists on the role of GM crop technologies

Participants expressed largely negative opinions on GM foods, not least because the technology was seen as benefiting the producer, not the consumer

23

Table 1. Factors shaping the controversy over GM crops

Country	Perceived authority of the regulatory agencies	Cultural resonance of the crop
Mexico GM maize	Low Decisions by regulatory bodies seen as lacking in authority and transparency and judged at times to be illegal	High Maize is an integral part of Mexican identity, history and culture
Brazil GM soya	Low/Medium Approvals have been successfully authorised by the National Technical Commission for Biosecurity (CTNBio) since 2005, leading to widespread planting, but decisions remain contested	Low Soya has little cultural significance in Brazil
India GM cotton	Low Regulatory bodies seen as lacking in transparency and capacity; perceived gaps in the regulatory system led to 2013 moratorium	High The fragile thread of cotton is a national symbol of Indian self-sufficiency

in providing significant future agricultural advances, emphasising economic benefits, the apparent unparalleled ability of GM crop technologies to provide improvements and the necessity for agricultural GM research to have a strong national base. In our research with the urban lay public in Florianopolis, we found little knowledge or awareness of GM crops and foods and genuine surprise about the extent of their adoption. Notwithstanding a general trust in science, participants expressed largely negative opinions on GM foods, not least because the technology was seen as benefiting the producer, not the consumer, and because they had not been consulted or clearly informed.

Intensity of protest movements	Genetic modification as symbol of wider struggle	Degree of public engagement
High The anti-GM campaign has sustained its presence since 2002	**High** GM maize is a symbol of the protest against neoliberalism and the North American Free Trade Agreement (NAFTA)	**Low** There has been little sustained effort by institutional actors to engage the public
High until 2003 **Low** from 2005 Following the passing of the Biosafety Law the protests peter out	**High** until 2003, with GM crops situated within an anti-globalisation discourse **Low** from 2005	**Low** There has been little sustained effort by institutional actors to engage the public
High The anti-GM campaign has sustained high-profile protests	**High** *Bt* (insect-resistant) cotton is a symbol of the struggle against multinationals and neoliberalism	**Low** There has been little sustained effort by institutional actors to engage the public

In India, we found that GM cotton had become a provocative symbol of foreign control and imposition, where regulatory bodies have been routinely criticised for using inadequate procedures for the approval of GM crops. In our ethnography of laboratory scientists, we found that those whose work we observed were opposed to the moratorium and constructed and perceived the position of anti-GM actors as "ignorant" or "publicity seeking". Scientists' critique of the moratorium was often framed in post-colonial language, as they argued that India could not afford the risk of falling behind in the development of biotechnology. In research with groups of lay people, we found the majority of our participants to have developed negative views on GM crops and foods,

The key factors explaining the controversy over GM crops are social and institutional in nature with city dwellers emphasising their mistrust of governmental and local-authority capacity to provide a reliable regulatory system, and with rural participants arguing that using GM seeds was interfering with the preservation of indigenous seeds.

Across all three case studies, we found that the technical regulatory bodies responsible for approvals for the release of GM crops had not provided "authoritative governance",[3] that the predominant research culture in national biotechnology laboratories had little capacity to respond to wider societal responsibilities, and that lay people broadly tended to adopt negative views when introduced to the technology and its application. To summarise, we found that the key factors explaining the controversy over GM crops are social and institutional in nature, and transcend questions of technical risk. These are presented in Table 1.

Responding to this "institutional void", we proposed a novel way to govern GM crops informed by recent debates on responsible innovation:[4] if we are to innovate responsibly and robustly, we need new institutional capacities to better anticipate the wider driving forces as well as impacts of emerging technologies, and we need to open up an inclusive debate with stakeholders and the wider public, to develop more reflexive scientific cultures and to develop new governance architectures that are responsive to these processes. The responsible innovation framework has been pioneered in UK research and is being implemented by UK research councils[5] and more widely across Europe. It offers new potential to reconfigure the debate on the governance of GM foods and crops in the UK, in Europe and internationally, and hopefully to help move the debate away from its current polemic and impasse.

References

1. **Macnaghten, P., Carro-Ripalda, S. and Burity, J. (eds.) (2014).** *A New Approach to Governing GM Crops: Global Lessons from the Rising Powers.* Durham University Working Paper, Durham, UK. http://bit.ly/1p957cb (Accessed 20 January 2015).

2. **Macnaghten, P. and Carro-Ripalda, S. (eds.) (2015** forthcoming). *Governing Agricultural Sustainability: Global Lessons from GM Crops.* Routledge, London, UK.

3. **Hajer, M. (2009).** *Authoritative Governance: Policy-making in the Age of Mediatization.* Oxford University Press, Oxford, UK.

4. **Stilgoe, J., Owen, R. and Macnaghten, P. (2013).** Developing a framework of responsible innovation, *Research Policy* 42: 1568–1580.

5. **EPSRC (2013).** *Framework for Responsible Innovation.* Engineering and Physical Science Research Council. https://www.epsrc.ac.uk/research/ framework (Accessed 20 January 2015).

Authors

Dr Phil Macnaghten, Professor in the Department of Social Sciences, Wageningen University, Netherlands
Dr Susana Carro-Ripalda, Core Investigator and Project Manager, Department of Anthropology, University of Durham, UK

Can GM crops help African farmers? Insights from Uganda

Matthew A. Schnurr, Lincoln Addison,
Sarah Mujabi-Mujuzi and Tonny Miiro

C an genetically modified (GM) crops help African farmers improve yields
and livelihoods? This project aimed to answer this question by bringing
to the fore the perspectives of more than 250 smallholder farmers in Uganda,
a country with one of the largest experimental programmes dedicated to
agricultural biotechnology on the continent.

Much of the enthusiasm around the potential for GM crops to alleviate poverty
and hunger in Uganda revolves around the country's primary carbohydrate
staple, the East African highland banana. Known locally as *matooke*, this
banana is not eaten raw but rather peeled, boiled, mashed and then wrapped
in banana leaves and stewed in a pot set over a fire, creating a soft mash with
a vibrant yellow colour. *Matooke* is by far the most important crop in Uganda,
accounting for more than a third of the country's daily caloric intake.

It is difficult to overestimate the degree to which environmental scourges impede the nation's production of its primary staple crop

Current experimental trials are developing
a strain of *matooke* that is genetically
modified to resist the crop's most pernicious pests, such as nematodes and
weevils, and diseases including banana
bacterial wilt (BBW), black Sigatoka and

Fusarium wilt. There is also a separate experimental line using genetic modification to biofortify the crop, increasing its Vitamin A content in order to reduce maternal and infant mortality. It is

Previous efforts at enhancing resistance through conventional breeding yielded few results, hindered by crop characteristics and cultural preferences

difficult to overestimate the degree to which environmental scourges impede the nation's *matooke* production: the most pressing of these, BBW, is projected to cause losses of US$ 4–8 billion over the coming decade.[1]

Previous efforts at enhancing resistance through conventional breeding yielded few results, hindered both by crop characteristics – banana is predominantly sterile, with a long generation time – and cultural preferences: progress with interbreeding wild races that demonstrate resistance to pests and diseases has largely been rejected by consumers due to dissatisfaction with taste and texture. These constraints have convinced breeders in Uganda's National Agricultural Research Organization (NARO) that genetic modification presents the most promising means of ensuring *matooke*'s long-term sustainable production. Many observers expect the first GM version of *matooke* to be ready as early as 2017, though it is important to note that no GM varieties can be released until the Ugandan parliament has passed legislation allowing for commercialisation.

This project investigated farmer attitudes and intentions to adopt GM versions of *matooke* banana. There is a great need for diagnostic research that analyses attitudes towards GM crops before they are commercially released, as these are the major predictors for both adoption rates and use intensities. Probing attitudes is crucial to predicting how farmers will react to these technologies once they are released and the extent to which they will transform agricultural production.[2] Thus these research findings make an important contribution to the scholarly debate over whether GM versions of African carbohydrate staple crops can improve agricultural production among the continent's smallholder farmers.

The research objectives of this project were threefold:

1. Evaluate farmer attitudes to GM varieties of *matooke* banana currently under experimentation.
2. Assess whether this technology can help farmers to improve yields and livelihoods.
3. Bring to light farmers' perspectives on these soon-to-be-released technologies.

We sought to realise these objectives by using both random and purposive techniques to create a sample that could accurately reflect farmer perspectives on these emerging technologies. Our starting point was the country's most recent Census of Agriculture, which revealed that the vast majority of *matooke* banana growers were unevenly spread across three major growing regions, with 15 per cent in the eastern region, 35 per cent in the central region, and 50 per cent in the southwestern region. We set out to generate a data set that reflected this geographical distribution. Districts were randomly selected based on an updated list provided by the more recent national census. A random number generator was then used to select sub-counties, parishes,

The more commercially oriented farmers, with larger farms, better information and larger networks, are most likely to hold positive attitudes to genetic modification

villages and individual households. Certain districts and sub-counties had to be excluded for reasons of health and safety as well as inaccessibility during the rainy season.

Our findings cast doubt on whether GM matooke will benefit the country's poorest and most vulnerable farmers

More than 170 farmers from across the three major growing regions participated in a progression of quantitative exercises, which relied heavily on visual aids and side-by-side comparisons, designed to bridge the gap between hypothetical exercises and farm-level realities. These exercises aim to depict the implications of BBW-resistant and biofortified GM banana in order to capture farmer responses and reactions to these soon-to-be-released varieties. A further 100 farmers participated in qualitative methods including focus groups and video diaries designed to probe why farmers feel the way they do about these emerging technologies. Sampling for these qualitative methods was designed to maximise heterogeneous characteristics including age, education, gender and farm size.

We produced research results that speak directly to the project's three research objectives. With respect to the first objective, we used non-parametric statistical tests to determine which socio-economic factors influenced farmer attitudes towards GM *matooke* varieties. Five were statistically significant in shaping farmers' intentions to adopt: region, farm size, membership of a farmers' association, previous experience with improved varieties, and visits from agricultural extension workers. Our results indicate that the more market- and commercially oriented farmers in the southwest region, with larger farms, better information and larger networks, are most likely to hold positive attitudes to GM *matooke*.

31

Appropriate technology is sorely needed in Africa, but this has to be understood as one critical element of a broader package of agricultural development

With respect to the second research objective, our findings cast doubt on whether GM *matooke* will benefit the country's poorest and most vulnerable farmers. Three results are relevant here. First, there is a disconnect between the first GM variety scheduled to be released (the biofortified version with increased Vitamin A content) and the agronomic characteristics that farmers would prefer to see prioritised, which revolve primarily around pest and disease resistance. This suggests that the traits given precedence in the experimental programmes do not accurately reflect farmers' needs. Second, data reveal that the increased cost of GM *matooke* could prove to be a barrier to adoption, particularly among the poor, with research scientists estimating that GM planting materials could cost four times as much as non-GM versions. Third, our findings reveal that a major obstacle to uptake might have nothing to do with the GM technology itself but relate to the variety into which it is inserted, one which is considered unpopular among growers because of its unappealing texture and small fruit.

With respect to the third research objective, this project allowed for the development of methods for talking *with* rather than talking *to* farmers about the prospects of GM *matooke*. Community meetings and policy workshops brought together major stakeholders and offered a forum for farmers to voice their perspectives on the potential advantages and disadvantages of GM technology, though these outreach activities also underlined the crucial power relations that preclude farmers from playing a meaningful role in shaping agricultural development decisions.

Two policy recommendations emerge from these results. First, identifying the key variables that shape attitudes and intentions to adopt – including region, farm size, farmers' association membership, experience with improved varieties and agricultural extension workers' visits – offers a promising means for policy makers to target demographic pockets of early adopters. Our results suggest that the roll-out should start with the larger, more market-oriented farmers in the southwest region, who appear most enthusiastic about these new varieties. Also, policy makers should aim to capitalise on existing farmers' associations, adopters of improved varieties and relationships with extension agents, as farmers who already have experience of and exposure to new knowledge and technologies through these networks seem more willing to embrace GM versions of *matooke*.

The second policy insight is more cautionary. The five variables that significantly impact attitudes and intentions to adopt are all associated with affluence and influence. These results thus raise important questions about the potential for GM *matooke* to help the poorest and most vulnerable in the country; that is, those who are disproportionately located in the eastern and central region, with smaller farms, who tend to be excluded from formalised social networks and lack critical access to information. The current prioritisation of biofortified varieties, high costs associated with initial release and choice of a host variety lacking in popularity raise concerns about whether these varieties will be able to help the segments of the population that need it most.

More generally, our conversations with farmers reinforce the message that new

Any investment in new GM varieties without concomitant investment in addressing structural dynamics is destined to fail

33

Whether or not a GM version of an African carbohydrate staple crop can achieve its stated goal depends on the circumstances faced by farmers on the ground

breeding technologies alone are insufficient to alter the continent's future agricultural production.

Appropriate technology is sorely needed in Africa, but this has to be understood as one critical element of a broader package of agricultural development. Farmers were consistent in describing their agricultural requirements holistically, vocalising the need for improved varieties alongside access to markets, the availability of credit, better information, enhanced extension services and adequate storage. Any investment in new GM varieties without concomitant investment in addressing these structural dynamics is destined to fail.

In conclusion, this research is a reminder that any analysis of whether a GM version of an African carbohydrate staple crop can achieve its stated goal of alleviating poverty and hunger for poor farmers depends on the specific circumstances faced by farmers on the ground. Many of the arguments in favour of GM crops hinge upon a separation of technology and context, which assumes that a single technology can succeed in effecting change within vastly different settings across the continent. But assessing the potential impact of these technologies requires situating them within the particular ecological, political and social contexts in which they are expected to succeed. To move beyond the polarized pro- versus anti- debate, we need more grounded, empirical studies of whether a particular GM trait and crop makes sense in a particular place. After all, it is the continent's farmers who will decide whether GM crops will emerge as a fixture of African agricultural production.

References
1. **IRIN (2009).** *East Africa: Banana Blight Puts Livelihoods at Risk.* UN Office for the Coordination of Humanitarian Affairs. http://www.irinnews.org/report/84873/east-africa-banana-blight-puts-livelihoods-at-risk (Accessed 5 January 2014).
2. **Hall, C. (2008).** Identifying farmer attitudes towards genetically modified (GM) crops in Scotland: Are they pro- or anti-GM? *Geoforum* 39: 204–212.

Authors
Dr Matthew A. Schnurr, Associate Professor, Department of International Development Studies, Dalhousie University, Halifax, USA
Dr Lincoln Addison, Post Doctoral Fellow, Department of International Development Studies, Dalhousie University, Halifax, USA
Sarah Mujabi-Mujuzi, independent professional working with governments, farming communities and non-state actors on issues of agricultural development, food security and nutrition
Tonny Miiro, Graduate Student, University of Queensland, Australia

Adoption of GM crops in Africa: why the seed sector matters

Edward Mabaya

The adoption of genetically modified (GM) crops in Africa has been slow and highly controversial. Most of Africa's 53 countries are at various stages of creating policy and regulatory frameworks that would allow GM crop research and commercialisation, but to date only four – Burkina Faso, Egypt, Sudan and South Africa – have fully commercialised GM crops, and five further countries – Cameroon, Kenya, Malawi, Nigeria and Uganda – are currently conducting field trials, the final step before full approval for commercialisation.[1] At the same time, however, there is growing public opposition to GM crops in Africa, best described as a fear of the unknown. For example, the import of GM foods is currently banned in Angola, Ethiopia, Kenya, Lesotho, Madagascar, Malawi, Mozambique, Swaziland, Tanzania, Zambia and Zimbabwe.

To evaluate the potential of GM crops in Africa, most studies have focused on consumer acceptance and farmers' willingness to pay. The central premise of the current chapter is that decisions made by Africa's seed sector – including private seed companies, government agencies, research institutions and non-governmental organisations (NGOs) involved in the research, production, regulation and dissemination of seeds in Africa – is likely to determine if, when, where and how GM crops are commercialised. With a focus on Africa's

There is growing public opposition to GM crops in Africa, best described as a fear of the unknown

seed sector, the current chapter summarises research findings on the following three interrelated questions:

1. How developed is the formal seed sector in Africa?
2. How does the level of seed sector development affect the adoption of GM crops?
3. What are the views of seed industry professionals on GM crops?

How developed is the formal seed sector in Africa?

Access to affordable, high-quality and locally adapted improved seed has long been recognised as critical to improving agricultural productivity among smallholder farmers in Africa. Yet seed systems in most African countries are still relatively underdeveloped, with improved seed accounting for approximately 20 per cent of planted seeds compared with a worldwide average of 65 per cent.[2,3,4]

A 2013 study on the status of seed systems development in Sub-Saharan Africa paints a complex picture of Africa's seed sector.[4] First, formal seed systems in Sub-Saharan Africa are highly fragmented (Figure 1). Africa's seed sector involves numerous players, sometimes with conflicting interests, operating in a loosely integrated value chain. Compared to other regions of the world where the seed sector is highly vertically integrated, the fragmented structure of the African seed sector slows the speed of technology diffusion, including of hybrid and GM crops. Adding to this complexity is the fact that the industry structure and its participants' conduct are ever-evolving to cope with the dynamic macro-

Access to high-quality, locally adapted, improved seed at affordable prices has long been recognised as critical to improving agricultural productivity

Figure 1. Fragmented structure of Africa's formal seed sector slows technology diffusion

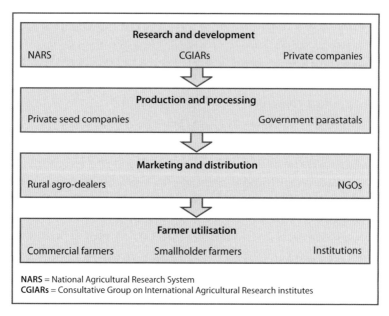

environment, which includes changes in seed policy and regulations, climate change, donor initiatives and advocacy put forward by special interest groups.

Another key finding from the same study is that Sub-Saharan Africa's formal seed sector is at different phases of development and structural transformation in different countries.[4] This finding is a key departure from the common narrative that often paints the continent's seed sector with one broad brush. The five phases of seed sector development that characterise most African countries are:

Phase 1: Nascent. Many African countries are still in the nascent or embryonic stages of seed sector development, wherein key policy and institutional frameworks for a formal seed sector are absent. The little seed that is available is imported and used almost exclusively by commercial farmers or relief programmes. Countries in this category include Angola, Democratic Republic of the Congo, Liberia, Sierra Leone, Somalia and South Sudan.

Phase 2: Emerging. Countries with emerging seed sectors often have some breeding programmes and a formalised variety release process supported by a basic policy and regulatory framework. Seed production and distribution is conducted by a handful of seed companies and/or government parastatals (organisations having some political authority and serving the state indirectly). Adoption of improved seed in these countries is limited to innovating farmers. Countries with an emerging seed sector include Botswana, Côte d'Ivoire, Mali, Madagascar, Mozambique, Niger, Rwanda and Senegal.

Phase 3: Early growth. With breeding programmes well established and seed policies still evolving, these countries are in transition to early growth. Start-up seed companies begin to produce and sell a limited range of staple crops to early-adopting farmers. Countries in the early growth stage include Burkina Faso, Ethiopia, Ghana, Nigeria and Tanzania. Both governments and NGOs are still significant players, supported by a growing agro-dealer network.

Phase 4: Late growth. Spurred by private companies, countries in the late-growth stage have well-established

The formal seed sectors in Sub-Saharan African countries are in different phases of development and structural transformation

39

seed sectors supported by an enabling environment. In this stage, private-sector participation is highly competitive, often with multinational and domestic seed companies producing a wide array of high-quality seeds distributed through a strong agro-dealer network. Only a handful of East and Southern African countries are in this stage, namely Kenya, Malawi, Uganda, Zambia and Zimbabwe.

Phase 5: Mature. This final stage of seed sector development is characterised by a self-regulating and fully privatised seed sector that is on a par with that of developed countries. Most participating companies are vertically integrated, with in-house breeding programmes and a tightly managed distribution system. In Sub-Saharan Africa, only South Africa has reached the mature stage. However, it should be noted that South Africa's seed sector has evolved primarily to serve large-scale commercial farmers while the needs of smallholder farmers remain underserved.[5]

How does the level of seed sector development affect GM crop adoption?
Widespread adoption of GM crops requires a well-functioning formal seed sector to efficiently produce and market affordable seeds as well as train smallholder farmers on proper stewardship. This is necessary because GM crops fall within the same operating environment and regulatory frameworks as conventionally bred crops. A study on the factors influencing the adoption of GM crops in Africa identifies the following critical factors: ministerial control of biosafety, peer country influence, stage of seed sector development, advocacy by key political figures, the media, activism, food security and technical capacity.[6]

A vibrant and well-established seed sector can be a key driving force for GM adoption

Figure 2. African countries' seed sector stage compared to GM crop application stage

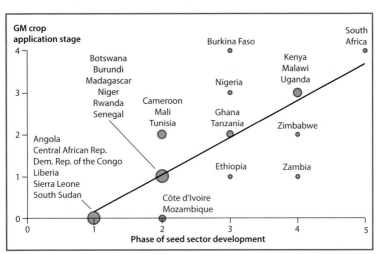

Mabaya *et al.* use the five-phase classification system discussed above to ana-lyse the impact of seed sector development on GM application and policy presence.[6] For this research, the GM application stage for each country was classified as follows: (0) no activity; (1) developing capacity for research and development (R&D); (2) contained research; (3) contained field trials; and (4) commercial release.

As illustrated in Figure 2, there is a strong positive correlation between a country's progress towards adopting GM crops and the stage of seed sector development. None of the countries with nascent seed sectors have made any progress towards GM crop adoption. In contrast, countries with the most advanced sectors (phases 4 and 5) all have biotechnology policies in place.

Those in the early phases (2 and 3) have the highest rates of GM policy in draft form. It is evident from this trend that a vibrant and well-established seed sector can be a key driving force for GM adoption. The study concludes that adoption of improved seed varieties, as manifested in a country's stage of seed sector development, results in an increase in demand for productivity-enhancing technologies and thereby drives support for GM crops.[6] There are, however, a few exceptions to this pattern, such as Burkina Faso and Sudan, which have commercialised Bt (insect-resistant) cotton even though they have less developed seed sectors.

What do African seed sector representatives think of GM crops?
Another study by Mabaya and Fulton explored attitudes towards GM crops among the leaders of the continent's seed sector, including private seed companies, government agencies, research institutions and NGOs involved in the research, production, regulation and dissemination of seeds in Africa.[7] Based on an industry survey of more than 320 respondents across Africa conducted in 2012 and 2013, the Mabaya and Fulton study reveals a strong acceptance of biotechnology among seed sector experts across the continent. Table 1 shows the distribution of responses to some key statements on GM crops, with the most frequent responses highlighted in bold.

Unless and until the formal seed sector develops to a level that can deliver conventional hybrid seed to most smallholder farmers, the GM debate will remain just that

While participants in the survey generally had an informed and positive view about GM crops, there were some notable differences of opinion. Some of these were based on the home country's level of seed sector development and the stated

Table 1. Survey results

Statement	Reaction to statement, %				
	Strongly agree	Agree	Neither	Disagree	Strongly disagree
1. GM crops have the potential to improve Africans' food security	36.4	**44.5**	8.1	7.2	3.7
2. African governments should enact stricter regulations on GM crops	15.0	**37.7**	18.4	21.5	7.5
3. Products containing GM crop ingredients should be labelled as "Containing Genetically Engineered Ingredients"	38.3	**38.9**	10.3	7.8	4.7
4. I would buy food that I know contains GM crop ingredients	20.6	**46.6**	17.2	10.6	5.0
5. Smallholder farmers in Africa will benefit from planting GM crops	26.8	**41.4**	16.5	9.7	5.6
6. Food containing GM crops will cause harm to those who consume them	1.6	6.0	30.4	**37.9**	24.1
7. The potential benefits of GM crops outweigh the risks	21.5	**41.1**	26.9	8.5	1.9

knowledge of GM crops: the more developed a respondent's country's seed sector, the more beneficially GM crops were perceived. An undeveloped seed sector appears to limit the knowledge and awareness of GM crops and thus they are seen less as a tool to improve food security. In addition, those with a knowledge of GM crops were more positive about the technology. However, there was not much difference between the responses of those who worked in the private sector and those from the public sector. Overall, those experts involved in the seed sector who were surveyed were strong proponents of GM technology. The support for modern biotechnology was even stronger for non-food crops such as *Bt* cotton and tobacco.

Conclusion

Africa has been slow in adopting GM crops. In most countries, both political debate and public opinion have been shaped by a fear of the unknown fuelled by social media. However, the potential of GM crops to improve food security on the African continent will depend, to a large extent, on the role of the seed sector. Unfortunately, the formal seed sector in most countries is in the very early phases of development. Farmers and policy makers need to appreciate the value of improved seed before they can appreciate GM crops. It is encouraging that seed sector professionals in Africa see the potential for GM crops to improve the continent's food security. In the right enabling environment, the seed sector can trigger a domino effect among other stakeholders in favour of GM crop commercialisation.

Lest we forget, GM crops can only get to farmers through the seed system. Unless and until the formal seed sector develops to a level that can deliver conventional hybrid seed to most smallholder farmers, the GM debate will remain just that. If GM crops become an essential tool for improving food security in Africa, the seed sector will be the vehicle that delivers the tool to smallholder farmers.

References

1. **Abidoye, A.O. and Mabaya, E. (2014).** Adoption of genetically modified crops in South Africa: Effects on wholesale maize prices, *Agrekon: Agricultural Economics Research, Policy and Practice in Southern Africa* 53(1): 104–123.
2. **Langyintuo, A., Mwangi, W., Diallo, A.O., MacRobert, J., Dixon, J. and Banziger, M. (2008).** *An Analysis of the Bottlenecks Affecting the Production and Deployment of Maize Seed in Eastern and Southern Africa.* International Maize and Wheat Improvement Center (CIMMYT), Harare, Zimbabwe.
3. **Tahirou, A., Sanogo, D., Langyintuo, A., Bamire, S.A. and Olanrewaju, A. (2009).** *Assessing the Constraints Affecting Production and Deployment of Maize Seed in DTMA Countries of West Africa.* International Institute of Tropical Agriculture (IITA), Ibadan, Nigeria.
4. **Mabaya, E., Omanga, P. and DeVries, J. (2013).** Status of seed systems development in Sub-Saharan Africa, in: *Africa Agriculture Status Report: Focus on Staple Crops.* Alliance for Green Revolution in Africa (AGRA), Nairobi, Kenya, pp. 53–68.
5. **TASAI** (The African Seed Access Index), South Africa brief, available online at www.tasai.org (Accessed March 2015).
6. **Mabaya, E., Fulton, J., Simiyu-Wafukho, S. and Nang'ayo, F. (2015).** Factors influencing adoption of genetically modified crops in Africa, *Development Southern Africa* 32(5): 577–591.
7. **Mabaya, E. and Fulton, J. (2015).** *Attitudes towards Genetically Modified Crops in Africa: A Seed Industry Perspective,* under review.

Author

Dr Edward Mabaya, Associate Director, Cornell International Institute for Food, Agriculture and Development, Cornell University, USA

Using a Community of Practice to learn from smallholders in South Africa

Mary K. Hendrickson, Jere L. Gilles,
William H. Meyers, Kenneth C. Schneeberger
and William R. Folk

Genetically modified (GM) maize has been used by commercial farmers in South Africa since 1998, but evidence of its use by small-holder subsistence farmers is lacking. Some 40 per cent of South Africa's subsistence producers farm in KwaZulu-Natal (KZN) province, so this was an appropriate place for a Community of Practice (CoP) to examine the conditions under which GM crops could be used by smallholders and gain insights on the appropriateness of these technologies for them as well as for smallholders in other contexts.

Over the course of two cropping seasons (2012–2014), three groups of smallholders used GM maize and, through the CoP, interacted with leaders of the provincial farmer's organisation Kwanalu,[1] input suppliers, non-governmental organisations (NGOs), researchers and government officials. By putting smallholders first we found that they were enthusiastic about the benefits of GM maize, particularly for saving labour through weed control. However, we found their knowledge of the difference between traditional maize varieties and hybrid and GM

By putting smallholders first we found that they were enthusiastic about the benefits of GM maize

varieties to be limited. We also found that smallholders appreciated workshops and training in better maize production techniques, particularly in managing soil fertility, and that they could benefit from the development of improved market, transport and storage infrastructure.

Community of Practice

CoP is a co-learning environment created by researchers, educators and smallholders (Table 1), who can analyse technologies and organise knowledge systems in a way that avoids the unintended negative consequences that often accompany traditional technology transfer. For this project, the CoP connected smallholders, researchers, educators and community members possessing different sets of knowledge and practice. Each group evaluated potential innovations from their own perspective, and all worked together to develop solutions through regular interaction. In forming the CoP in KZN, we built on Kwanalu's long-standing relationship with the farmers who became part of this project. While many of the non-farmer participants in the CoP had used participatory methods before, our CoP was a new experience for them

Table 1. Members of the Community of Practice

Sector	Organisations/institutions
Smallholders	Members of farmer associations from Dannhauser, Estcourt and Hlanganani
Researchers	Agricultural Research Council, University of KZN, KZN Department of Agriculture (Cedara), University of Missouri
NGOs	Kwanalu, Grain SA, Lima and Farmer Support Group
Private business	Monsanto and Pannar (seed companies)
Government	Extension educators from the provincial Department of Agriculture

Table 2. Laboratory testing for the presence of GM traits in maize germplasm and meal

Variety	Test for GM
Open pollinated (commonly available smallholder variety)	3 No, 2 Yes
Hybrid (commonly available)	1 No, 4 Yes
GM	5 Yes
Maize meal (purchased at supermarkets)	All tested positive

Note: Maize kernels were obtained from the farms of smallholders expressing interest in participating in the CoP in each of the three locations, while maize meal was purchased from supermarkets in Pietermaritzburg and surrounding towns at the beginning of our research. Laboratory analysis was done at the University of Missouri, Division of Biochemistry.

because it put smallholders at the forefront. This strengthened farmers' voices in the process of technology adoption and influenced the behaviour and decision making of other stakeholders.

We also collected data about the presence of GM traits in the maize germplasm used by smallholders in the project areas, as well as in commercially available maize meal (Table 2). Given that genetic modification has already been in widespread use among the commercial farmers who produce more than 90 per cent of the province's maize crop, GM traits were expected to be present in both meal and open-pollinated varieties. These results, as well as our reports about South African consumer impressions of GM maize and prior smallholder experience with GM crops, contributed to our database of literature and information on the use of GM crops among South African smallholders. This information is now available through our Community Commons hub (www.communitycommons.org/groups).

Prior to establishing the CoP, members of the University of Missouri team visited commercial and smallholder farmer-members of Kwanalu and learned that the smallholders were unable to participate fully in discussions about GM crops because of their lack of experience of the technology, financial constraints and poor access to the inputs necessary for commercial maize production. They also had a limited voice in local or provincial government decisions. Based on these visits, we selected three different areas of KZN in which to establish demonstration trials with smallholder members of farmer associations.

At each site, seed from conventional hybrids, *Bt* (insect-resistant) and HT (herbicide-tolerant) maize was provided by project personnel for smallholders to plant in a demonstration plot that also included the type of seed that they normally used – generally open-pollinated varieties. Activities included workshops with all participants to explain the CoP and to develop plans for demonstration trials. Over two planting seasons, smallholders received training on soil fertility, maize production systems, weed management and seed varieties. In the second season, a no-till plot – leaving the soil undisturbed by tilling – and stacked GM maize carrying both insect-resistance and herbicide-tolerance genes, were included in the trials. Additional activities included planting days, tastings of green mealies (immature maize as roasting ears), harvest days and debriefing on the knowledge smallholders had gained from the trials.

Smallholders' plans to cultivate GM maize may be difficult to implement ... access to inputs is limited and chaotic

Additionally, we hosted two conferences attended by smallholders, non-farmer stakeholders and interested parties from

49

Given the difficulty of storage and transport to markets, the economic benefits of GM maize may be limited to what local markets can absorb

NGOs, the University of KZN and the Department of Agriculture. These conferences helped non-farmer stakeholders and others understand the smallholders' experiences with GM crops. Some 75 farmers and a dozen or more non-farmers participated over the course of the CoP.

What did we learn?

Despite the long history of GM crops in South Africa, there was little comprehension of GM technology among smallholders. During pre-planting visits, smallholders were specifically asked about their experience and knowledge of genetic modification, and only one group expressed an understanding of the differences between GM, hybrid and open-pollinated seeds. Their leader was very knowledgeable about maize production and often interacted with commercial farmers and seed company representatives, but questions asked by group members suggested that this awareness was not shared by all. Most smallholders in the CoP were confused about the differences between seed types, such as open-pollinated varieties and hybrids with or without GM traits, and were unaware that GM seeds were used in nearby fields. Despite this, GM crops, especially with herbicide-tolerance traits, were enthusiastically embraced because of significant issues with labour and weed management. Much to the surprise of non-farmer stakeholders, smallholders indicated that they would continue to try to acquire and plant GM maize.

These plans may be difficult to implement, however. Access to inputs is limited and chaotic. Seed distribution happens in two primary ways: municipalities supply free seeds and other inputs to recognised farmer associations, or smallholders purchase seed on their own through a network of agricultural input stores. Smallholders noted that they often buy the cheapest seeds and fertilisers, and just ask shopkeepers for yellow or white maize. Shops stock only what the seed suppliers provide and have difficulty regularly procuring seeds that meet the needs of smallholders. Given the difficulty of storage and transport to markets, the economic benefits of GM maize may be limited to what local markets can absorb.

Project outcomes

Smallholder farmers showed consistent learning through the CoP process, from fertility management to weed management to differences between GM, hybrid and conventional seeds. For instance, one group realised they had been over-applying fertiliser because they had never understood soil testing and the interpretation of results, while in another group some subsequently found the money to buy backpack sprayers in order to use herbicides. In addition, smallholders have accessed new networks by meeting with researchers and resource providers and by joining Grain SA, an association of grain farmers focused on improving grain production methods.

Another significant outcome was the foundation laid for future cooperation between Kwanalu and other organisations serving smallholders in KZN. Sandy LaMarque, Chief Executive of Kwanalu, expressed satisfaction that their organisation had a better understanding of the wants and needs of smallholders as a whole, not just in terms of their access to GM maize. Kwanalu and Lima, a rural development

The CoP's emphasis on putting smallholders and researchers in a co-learning environment resonates beyond the project

51

"I've learned that once the farmers are organised they can go far" organisation, have again partnered on a Rural Development Desk, in part due to their experiences of this CoP.

It is also clear that the CoP facilitated non-farmer stakeholders to learn from smallholders. Many stakeholders noted with surprise that smallholders are interested in GM seed or weed management, and have come to realise the holistic nature – from both the production and marketing side – of the issues facing smallholders. For instance, an extension provider observed: "The farmers are involved … and it is better than just planting and showing them what they must see. Here they are involved and must decide for themselves." A stakeholder from agribusiness said that the CoP helped him look at the whole smallholder system and that his company may have to make changes now because "they will know why the farmers are doing what they do".

Conclusion

The CoP's emphasis on putting smallholders and researchers in a co-learning environment resonates beyond the project. For instance, researchers from the University of Pretoria have proposed working with one of the communities for three to five years on maize virus diseases. While some view a CoP as time-intensive, it is doubtful that a demonstration trial alone would have built such relationships between smallholders, organisations and resources, or encouraged the networking that we have seen from this project. Moreover, as one of the authors noted, the CoP showed the importance of involving a whole range of stakeholders who help shape the context in which technology is deployed, particularly because it is easy as researchers to assume a pre-packaged solution to complex problems.

We close with how the CoP lifted up the voices of smallholders in our project. An extension provider said: "I've learned that once the farmers are organised they can go far." The CoP has given farmers both organisation and a voice about their farming needs.

As a rural development stakeholder noted, the CoP "has been done in an open environment of sharing without being overly prescriptive and in a non-arrogant and non-authoritative environment where the farmers are at the front of that decision-making system. You have created a very participatory environment and the relationships between stakeholders smell very strongly of equality."

Note
1. In 1997, Kwanalu emerged from the merger of the 107-year-old Natal Agricultural Union, which represented white commercial farmers, with the Madadeni Branch of the National African Farmers Union and the South Coast Indian Farmers Association.

Authors
Dr Mary K. Hendrickson, Assistant Professor, Department of Rural Sociology, Advisor Chair – Sustainable Agriculture, College of Agriculture, Food and Natural Resources (CAFNR), University of Missouri, Columbia, USA
Dr Jere L. Gilles, Associate Professor, Department of Rural Sociology, University of Missouri, Columbia, USA
Dr William H. Meyers, Director, CAFNR International Programs and Howard Cowden Professor of Agricultural and Applied Economics, College of Agriculture, Food and Natural Resources (CAFNR), University of Missouri, Columbia, USA
Dr Kenneth C. Schneeberger, International Training Coordinator, College of Agriculture, Food and Natural Resources (CAFNR), University of Missouri, Columbia, USA
Dr William R. Folk, Professor of Biochemistry, University of Missouri, Columbia, USA

Biotechnology regulatory systems: implications for food security and rural livelihoods

Samuel E. Timpo, Diran Makinde, Godwin N.Y. Lemgo,
Hashini G. Dissanayake, Joseph Guenthner
and Karim Maredia

The African Ministerial Conference on Science and Technology (AMCOST) in 2007 identified the application of modern biotechnology as having the potential to help address food, feed, fibre and fuel needs as well as contribute to combating diseases, malnutrition, hunger and poverty. This decision was taken against the backdrop that enhancing food security and livelihoods – despite growing populations, depleting natural resources and potential threats from climate change – was a major challenge confronting African governments and policy makers as well as international development agencies. It was noted that accessing and harnessing the potential of modern biotechnology would require well-trained human resources, appropriate infrastructure, knowledge-based innovations, financial mechanisms and functional regulatory systems.

Accessing and harnessing the potential of modern biotechnology requires well-trained human resources ... and functional regulatory systems

A functional regulatory system would enable the efficient and competent assessment of potential risks and benefits together with ensuring that regulatory decisions are made in a science-based, informed and timely manner. To this end, most African countries either acceded to, or ratified, the Cartagena Protocol on Biosafety, which seeks to guide parties in establishing functional regulatory systems that would enable a platform for the exchange of scientific and technical information and, ultimately, biosafety decision making. Although many African countries have developed some features of their biosafety systems for regulating agricultural biotechnology, to date only four countries – Burkina Faso, Egypt, South Africa and Sudan – commercially cultivate genetically engineered crops.

The nature of the problem

Today, many African countries have biotechnology policies, regulations and strategies, but then a look across the continent reveals limited capacity within national systems in regulatory decision making despite the efforts of a number of global, regional and sub-regional biosafety initiatives over the years. Observations by the New Partnership for Africa's Development (NEPAD) Agency's African Biosafety Network of Expertise (ABNE) indicated that significant variations in decision making exist between countries with apparently similar national regulatory systems. However, empirical evidence to explain these variations and to identify constraints that have impacted on the decision-making processes was lacking. Our study was therefore explanatory research aimed at understanding the issues that impair the functionality of biosafety systems as well as best practices that can be adapted by other countries in Africa. This was achieved by exploring the factors that influenced the differential ability of seven Sub-Saharan African countries to implement functional regulatory systems. Factors

Many African countries have biotechnology policies, regulations and strategies, but limited capacity in regulatory decision making

55

Countries that have made progress in the management of modern biotechnology have had enabling environments ... examined included the current state of regulatory capacity; the features that define agricultural biotechnology policy and biosafety regulatory regimes in the selected countries and their role in decision-making processes concerning genetically modified (GM) crops; countries' scientific and administrative capacity for risk assessment and risk management processes and procedures; and institutional arrangements for biosafety decision making.

Methodology

To understand the issues that affect the functionality of biosafety systems, qualitative surveys and desk reviews of official documents were used to obtain both primary and secondary data. A comparative case study methodology was used to analyse differences between the seven African countries selected from West Africa (Burkina Faso, Ghana and Nigeria), East Africa (Kenya and Uganda) and Southern Africa (Mozambique and South Africa) through the review of literature, multi-stakeholder surveys and focus group discussions. The target research population included regulators, scientists, industry practitioners, farmer-based organisations, consumer associations, non-governmental organisations, policy makers and decision makers. Cross-sectional data were used to further interpret the case studies and analysis of the different country scenarios. To achieve the desired mix, purposive sampling was employed to interview at least 30 respondents within each national system.

Key survey findings

Countries in Sub-Saharan Africa that have made progress in the management of modern biotechnology were found to have enabling environments –

regulatory and business-friendly – characterised by political will and a commitment to implement policy together with adequate legal authority, effective regulatory oversight roles and timeliness in regulatory processes. In such systems, biotechnology was identified as a development tool, and benefits from the use of the technology were weighed with risks in decision making. The risk assessment was a science-based or safety consideration and did not include socio-economic factors. The associated risk management measures proposed were commensurate with identified risks and likelihood of occurrence. However, socio-economic considerations and national priorities played a big role in the final decision making. The study also revealed that countries that delayed decision making did not quite understand the risk assessment process and often adopted an onerous approach. Risks thus were overemphasised, were associated with draconian provisions on liability and redress, and were also inappropriately linked to socio-economic considerations.

The study observed that within each regulatory system there were some influencers who positively or negatively contributed to regulatory processes depending on their viewpoints. These influencers, who operated either as individuals or groups, were not seen as target audiences for biosafety capacity strengthening, but turned out to be game changers in the evolution of regulatory systems towards functionality. They included politicians, local government leaders, community leaders, farmer groups, religious bodies and the

A key finding was the nuances of engaging with politicians to engender interest, cooperation and commitment, requiring an understanding of the politician's thought processes

media. These are powerful constituencies that have not necessarily been the focus of biosafety capacity building but which, when adequately informed, easily serve as biosafety champions. Countries that benefited from these supporters described the key attributes required of an impactful biosafety champion as:

- being politically connected and influential within the geopolitical space;
- being committed, involved and open to support from other team members;
- being blessed with a pleasant voice that resonates well in the ears of political leadership and catches their attention;
- having the ability to build bridges;
- being a good negotiator;
- understanding his/her role and able to discern relevance and timeliness;
- being imbued with a peripheral awareness enabling the seizure of opportunities that may periodically arise.

A key finding was the nuances of engaging with politicians to engender interest, cooperation and commitment. This requires an understanding of the politician's thought processes. Noting that political office is usually term-bound, most politicians will listen if they believe the message will further their political agenda. However, existing disconnects between science, technology and innovation (STI) on the one hand and livelihood issues such as food security, access to potable water and lives saved on the other have resulted in low interest and low prioritisation and commitment from politicians.

Most politicians will listen if they believe the message will further their political agenda

Regarding communicating STI issues with politicians, it was noted that messaging and message delivery were a challenge. Politicians were observed to visualise issues in an "anticlockwise" direction in that they would rather begin a conversation by discussing an exciting solution, only then moving on

Of the various areas of capacity-strengthening endeavours, biosafety communication was identified as the weakest link: there is a need for a communication rethink

to understand how it works and the reason for it. The classical model of identifying a problem, then stating the objectives, methodology and findings was unappealing to politicians who, given the limited time frame, were interested in practical and relevant solutions that they could share with the electorate. Countries where politicians positively supported biosafety processes, including enactment of the law and allocated budgets to support biosafety administrative processes, were those that perceived links to livelihood issues and, by extension, the socio-economic development agenda.

Of the various areas of capacity-strengthening endeavours – human resources, administrative handling of applications, risk assessment, decision making, communication and mechanisms for coordination – biosafety communication was identified as the key weakest link. There is a need for a communication rethink. This requires an effective strategy and a long-term approach including integrating biotechnology and biosafety into academic curricular, training science communicators and continuous public engagement. However, this public engagement must be conducted in a manner that ensures a clear distinction between biotechnology communication and biosafety communication. The study also revealed that myths and misperceptions that were not addressed within regulatory systems undermined

Better relationships were built through understanding and consulting stakeholders, ensuring clarity of roles and responsibilities, and having regular, open and transparent communication

later communication efforts. In addition, the public did not view biosafety as a subject matter that was compartmentalised into technical areas such as food safety, environmental safety and socio-economic considerations. Their concerns were usually a mixed bag of issues. Interactions with the media also revealed a dearth of engagement on various fronts, with media personnel pointing out that – unlike opponents of the technology – biosafety communicators scarcely provided the media with headline stories or information resources such as photographs.

The study also revealed that African countries have competent human resources that either go unrecognised or are placed in positions of little relevance to biosafety processes. For the competent personnel appropriately positioned within national systems, high turnovers and a lack of quality management systems in some regulatory systems were seen to undermine progress. There is a need for strategic and continuous capacity strengthening and dialogue to address these issues. Biosafety issues were observed to be like a jigsaw puzzle requiring a mix of strategies. Strategy development must be iterative, situational and dynamic. Domestically led processes ensured ownership and progress but this in part depended on partnerships to leverage resources for success. Some countries made strides with partners providing background technical support while stepping back from public view. Transparency, however, was an essential issue in building confidence in biosafety systems. Systems that made progress were engaged in multi-stakeholder involvement at critical steps, including decision making. Better relationships were built through understanding and consulting stakeholders, ensuring clarity of roles and responsibilities, and regular, open and transparent communication.

It is envisaged that the findings of this study will assist African regulators and policy makers to adopt policies and strategies to improve the efficiency of the biosafety decision-making process and reap the benefits of biotechnological advances while minimising the potential risks. This study will be an invaluable resource and a catalyst for increasing the number of functional regulatory systems across Africa, thus ensuring equitable access to good technology and sharing of benefits while protecting farmers, consumers and the environment. The project has been an important contribution to the NEPAD Agency's thematic programme on agriculture and food security.

Authors
Samuel E. Timpo, *Principal Investigator, NEPAD African Biosafety Network of Expertise, University of Ouagadougou, Burkina Faso*
Professor Diran Makinde, *Director, NEPAD African Biosafety Network of Expertise, University of Ouagadougou, Burkina Faso*
Godwin N.Y. Lemgo, *NEPAD African Biosafety Network of Expertise, University of Ouagadougou, Burkina Faso*
Dr Hashini G. Dissanayake, *Assistant Professor, Michigan State University, USA*
Dr Joseph Guenthner, *Professor in the Department of Agricultural Economics and Rural Sociology, Idaho State University, USA*
Dr Karim Maredia, *Professor and Program Director, World Technology Access (WorldTAP) Program of the Institute of International Agriculture and Department of Entomology, Michigan State University, USA*

Assessing and communicating the risks and benefits of GM cassava in Kenya

Harvey James, Corinne Valdivia, William R. Folk,
Dekha Sheikh, Festus Murithi, Violet Gathaara,
Milton Kengo, Charles Bett and Grace Mbure

K enya has yet to allow the commercialisation of genetically modified (GM) crop production,[1] so it is important to understand how small-holder farmers and other stakeholders would be affected if cassava, a major food security crop, were to be approved as a GM crop. To this end, scientists from the University of Missouri and the Kenya Agricultural and Livestock Research Organization (KALRO) conducted stakeholder interviews and developed a case study using participatory research methods in a two-year project between 2012 and 2014. The aim of the project was to answer two specific questions:

1. What are the intended and potential unintended consequences of introducing GM cassava in Kenya?

2. How can the risks and benefits of introducing GM cassava be com-municated to smallholders and other affected stakeholders?

Food security is a significant problem in Sub-Saharan Africa ... and cassava is part of the solution

Outcomes include understanding how the introduction of GM cassava might impact various stakeholders as well as identifying practical ways of involving stakeholders, especially women, in making informed decisions; describing the state of knowledge and shared interests to serve as a basis for groups who are in a position to influence policy; and developing strategies for communicating effectively to stakeholders the potential risks and benefits of introducing GM cassava. Recent studies of the state of bio-technology in Africa have identified these aspects as key needs.[2]

This chapter gives an overview of and conceptual foundation for the project, together with a summary of its key findings and conclusions.

Background

Cassava is an important food security crop for smallholder farmers in Sub-Saharan Africa. It can be stewed, boiled or processed into chips and flour, and its starch can be processed into tapioca and other food products, including flour. Cassava can also be used as a biofuel and animal feed. It is a drought-tolerant, low-input crop, and can remain unharvested for long periods of time. Food security is a significant problem in Sub-Saharan Africa for approximately one out of three people,[3] and cassava is unquestionably part of the solution. However, cassava production is threatened by two viruses: cassava mosaic disease (CMD) and cassava brown streak disease (CBSD). The Donald Danforth Plant Sciences Center in St Louis, Missouri, USA, in cooperation with KALRO, is developing a GM cassava resistant to both CMD and CBSD.[4]

There are two important factors affecting the debate about GM crops generally, and in Kenya specifically, which form an important basis for our study. The first involves the

Participatory approaches contribute to building knowledge, changing perceptions, identifying barriers and creating coalitions among stakeholders

63

Figure 1. Range of stakeholders expected to be affected by the introduction of GM cassava in Kenya

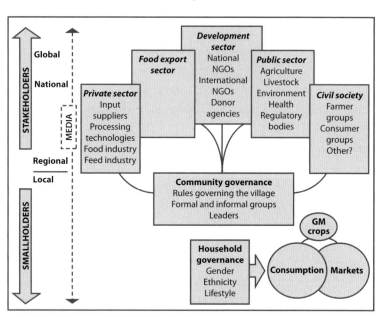

preferences and perspectives of stakeholders affected by the introduction of GM crops, especially smallholder farmers. The second is how the introduction of GM crops will affect smallholder farmers, other stakeholders and all members of society. Stakeholders include not only smallholders but other individuals and organisations in the community, national and international arenas (Figure 1). It is in this context that the introduction of GM cassava poses some risk. For example, the development of viral resistance to the GM traits can be predicted though the length of time required for it to emerge cannot. Consequently, if markets and the consumption of cassava are significantly altered, care must be taken to ensure that these altered markets are transitory and do not further destabilise food security in the event that the benefits of GM cassava are of short duration. Furthermore, the emergence of viral resistance could lead to increased risk of disease in the plants, as has been observed with gene silencing of papaya ringspot virus.[5]

The breadth of relationships between smallholders and other stakeholders exemplifies why multiple levels of stakeholders must be considered in this assessment, and the role of the media in affecting public perception of GM crops is significant.[6] It is important to identify these stakeholders and determine how they would be affected, especially those in a position to enable or veto the effective adoption of GM cassava by smallholders, and to engage them in dialogue.

Complicating the discussion is the fact that Kenya is diverse both socio-economically and culturally, with vast differences in urban and rural household consumption patterns, education, access to the media and culture, and the influence these may have. These differences affect the introduction of GM cassava at the household, community and national levels. No less significant are the key factors of gender and power status in and between households,[7] and their role in access to and control of resources.[8]

Conceptual foundations

The foundation for this protocol is built on a participatory research process and a sustainable livelihoods framework designed to better understand smallholder farmers, their contexts, livelihoods, concerns and capabilities, and how change increases vulnerability and leads to the growth or deterioration of human, natural, social, physical, economic and political capital. The framework is especially important in analysing how technology can impact the poor.[9] The approach is people-centred and focuses on both tangible and intangible assets and capabilities in developing livelihood strategies, especially in the context of negotiation with social, economic and political structures at the household, local, regional, national and international scales.[10, 11]

The participatory research method is one where farmers and researchers work together in a two-way communication process. Such approaches contribute to building knowledge, changing perceptions, identifying barriers, and creating coalitions among stakeholders to initiate change.[10] Power relations need to be addressed to ensure that community-based participatory planning processes include all people. Participation as a process seeks to empower through active participation, collaboration or partnership.[12] Gender and power relations are a central concern in agriculture, as women heads of household are often the most vulnerable.[7] Two-way communication is crucial to respecting people's right to be informed and make decisions regarding their livelihoods, and to building or strengthening social networks and human knowledge, as they are resources that foster alliances between key stakeholders and build trust in contexts of uncertainty such as GM technologies.[13]

The protocol

An effective protocol develops knowledge about the effects of adopting new technology and then communicates that knowledge to all relevant stakeholders, including smallholder farmers (Figure 2). The protocol is innovative in that a feedback process takes place as knowledge is developed.

An effective protocol develops knowledge ... and then communicates that knowledge to all relevant stakeholders

Figure 2. Communication protocol to build knowledge that enables two-way communication

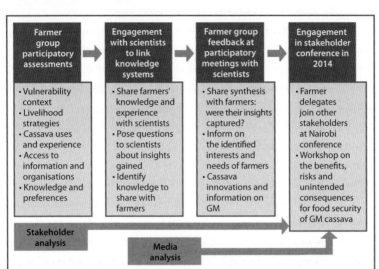

The participatory process centres on farmer focus groups. We selected two of KALRO's research centres in locations where cassava is a priority for our focus group discussions: Mtwapa, which is coastal and sub-humid, and Katumani in Machakos in the Eastern Province, which is characterised by dryland conditions. In the coastal region, cassava is consumed as a food security crop. In the Eastern Province, it has been identified as a crop with high potential for processing for markets. We invited smallholder farmers and community leaders from these communities to participate in the discussions and to complete a short questionnaire. Our sample included 115 farmers from the coast, including 82 women, and 94 farmers from the Eastern Province, including 57 women. Several techniques were employed to elicit information.

Participants appreciated that their knowledge and concerns were captured and addressed through feedback

Large group discussions led to the development of a timeline of the events that affect food security. The use of cards to capture the experiences of individual partici-pants allowed us to distinguish between vulnerable and non-vulnerable groups, and to assess the role of cassava and how its use differs for each group. Because many decisions on production, processing, consumption and market-ing vary between men and women, we also conducted focus groups addres-sing men and women separately so as to understand their vulnerabilities and coping methods, how integrated they were in the markets, how many organisations they used and which information they trusted.

We then engaged with more than 20 scientists and other stakeholders in semi-structured interviews in Kenya. This involved cassava scientists including those working with GM cassava, government officials in Kenya, representatives of non-governmental organisations (NGOs), and farmer groups associated with cassava production. The purpose of the interviews was to provide context and a baseline understanding for the focus group meetings with smallholder farmers. Interviews were transcribed with detailed notes but were not voice recorded.

We held a follow-up activity, termed farmer feedback session, at each site after the data from the focus groups were analysed. These sessions offered an oppor-tunity to share findings and research activities, confirm and ratify responses, answer questions about GM cassava and respond to the farmers' concerns about post-harvest processing and marketing. Scientists used leaflets, posters, videos, samples of healthy and diseased plants, and demonstrations on value-added products to share their research and expertise. Participants appreciated that their knowledge and concerns were captured during the process and addressed through feedback.[13]

Finally, we organised a stakeholder meeting in Nairobi in 2014, the purpose of which was to bring together farmers, scientists, policy makers and other stakeholders to discuss the potential risks, benefits and possible unintended consequences of introducing GM cassava in Kenya. The programme consisted of opening remarks and introductions, presentations of results and findings from the farmer feedback meetings, and a general discussion involving represented stakeholder groups about the challenges of meeting the food security needs of smallholder farmers and the potential benefits and concerns related to GM foods.

Lessons learned and knowledge created

Our general findings are that smallholder farmers are not well informed about GM crops but do not oppose their commercialisation. However, based on the small and differing pieces of information they receive, they have some concerns about the effects of GM crops when used for human consumption. Nonetheless, the more that farmers know about GM crops, the less concerned they are about the technology. Moreover, connectedness and access to information vary depending on degree of vulnerability. In this context, connectedness means having access to markets and information such as newspapers and extension agents. Vulnerability means being at greater risk in the case of extreme changes in weather, disease outbreaks, or other problems not faced by households

Smallholder farmers are generally not well informed about GM crops but do not oppose their commercialisation

69

Table 1. Summary of responses in Eastern Province regarding information about GM crops

Location	Have you heard about GM crops?	Where did you hear about GM crops?	Whom do you trust about GM crops?	What have you heard about GM crops?
Itithini	• 12 of 18 men • 6 of 27 women	• Farmers with a greenhouse • Newspaper stories about GM maize, which was to be imported	• Doctors who have assessed GM crops • Scientists from KALRO • Researchers • Officers from Ministry of Agriculture and Administration	• GM crops will be tested • GM crops do not cause cancer • One thing changed into another • Two plants crossed to make one
Mbuvo	• 4 of 19 men • 3 of 30 women	• Radio • Debate in parliament	• Scientists from KALRO	• Is not good • Is good for human consumption • Makes crops mature faster; will make humans age faster • Maize has been grafted like mangoes • Due to famine, used for family planning

with adequate reserves or sufficient cash to acquire food and meet their needs through market access. Farmers in less vulnerable groups are more connected, while those in more vulnerable groups are less connected.

Table 1 summarises findings about GM crops for farmers in two locations in Eastern Province. Farmers in Itithini engage in several risk-mitigating activities, such as selling baskets, wood carvings or sand, which makes them relatively more connected to markets and less vulnerable. Farmers in Mbuvo, in contrast, are more exposed to extreme weather conditions and are less connected to markets. The table shows that the degree to which farmers are connected and have access to information affects their perceptions about the risks and benefits of GM cassava and its adoption, with connectedness improving the quality of information farmers obtain and understand. While acknowledging that they do not have enough information to make definite decisions about the use of GM cassava, smallholder farmers indicated that the sources of information they would trust include researchers from KALRO and extension officers in the Ministry of Agriculture. Extension agents, however, are wary of the political will behind the introduction of GM crops. Moreover, because of the cultural significance of religion for Kenyans, the acceptability of GM crops among Christian and Muslim community leaders also matters, as we found from farmers in the coastal region.

Importantly, there are also gender differences in access to knowledge, types of connections to organisations and the level of assets, especially for vulnerable groups. For example, women who are connected have more access to self-help programmes than to institutions developing new technologies, while vulnerable men who are connected often lack the resources to act on new information.

Interestingly, decisions about the cassava varieties appropriate for production, processing and value addition are made by women, while harvesting and marketing in large quantities are often male activities.

Some farmers are concerned about the perception of cassava as a "poor man's crop", which they believe could affect its marketability

GM cassava has the potential to improve the livelihoods of smallholder farmers by providing crops free from disease and with improved nutrient content

There are also geographic differences. In Eastern Province, many farmers are connected to organisations seeking to foster the commercialisation of GM cassava. However, farmers are concerned about the perception of cassava as a "poor man's crop", which they believe could affect its marketability. In coastal regions where cassava is consumed as a food security crop, GM cassava would have to be the "right" variety – starchy, early maturing, not bitter, pest resistant and nutritious. Farmers are particular about the varieties of cassava they grow and consume. GM cassava that is clean – free from mosaic or brown streak disease – but that is not the type farmers traditionally use or need will not be accepted.

Scientists and other stakeholders believe that GM varieties of cassava will produce crops that are free from disease, resulting in higher yields, and will have greater nutritional content, thus improving the degree of food security for smallholders. However, increased productivity could alter the power relations between men and women, as more output might encourage men to sell the crops in markets, giving them – rather than women – access to much-needed cash. There is also concern about how GM cassava might affect management practices, since it is not clear that it can be incorporated into existing intercropping systems and because it requires a different set of farm inputs from those of conventionally grown cassava. An additional concern is the role of intellectual property rights. There are important social norms that support the sharing of clean cassava among Kenyan farmers, and there could be significant cultural repercussions if such norms are not respected when considering who controls access to GM crops in Kenya.

Summary

The introduction of GM cassava has the potential to improve the livelihoods of smallholder farmers by providing crops free from disease and with improved nutrient content. But there are risks, such as potential viral resistance and unforeseen changes in marketing and farm management practices, as described above. Accurate information about the benefits and risks associated with GM cassava need to be communicated to smallholder farmers and other stakeholders. An effective communication protocol translates knowledge in a way that takes account of the characteristics and context of the user. Thus, it requires a unique communication process which acknowledges that small-holder farmers' decisions, such as the choice to adopt GM crops, may also introduce risks that can threaten their ability to survive. In this context a two-way process makes it possible to develop and clarify knowledge that is trusted by smallholder farmers so that risks are minimised and smallholder livelihoods improved. It also acknowledges that farmers are often marginalised from mainstream institutions and often do not have a voice in the development of knowledge intended for their benefit.[13]

The communication approach as conceived and implemented in this project brought stakeholders together in ways that sought to strengthen the human, social and political capital of smallholder farmers as they engage with researchers and other involved parties. While women and men expressed their concerns about consuming more cassava, variety preferences and increasing pro-ductivity with no clear market

The communication approach in this project brought stakeholders together in ways that sought to strengthen the human, social and political capital of smallholder farmers

73

outlets, the research needs to focus on how to communicate about genetic modification, the farming practices and management approaches required, and what other stakeholders need to know, such as the consumption and environmental effects of introducing GM cassava in Kenya.

References
1. **Kameri-Mbote, P. (2011).** Regulation of GMO crops and foods: Kenya case study. Manuscript.
2. **Chambers, J.A., Zambrano, P., Falck-Zepeda, J., Gruere, G., Sengupta, D. and Hokanson, K. (2014).** *GM Agricultural Technologies for Africa: A State of Affairs.* African Development Group and International Food Policy Institute, Washington, DC, USA.
3. **Rosenthal, D.M. and Ort, D.R. (2012).** Examining cassava's potential to enhance food security under climate change, *Tropical Plant Biology* 5(1): 30–38.
4. **Taylor, N.J, Halsey, M., Gaitán-Solís, E., Anderson, P., Gichuki, S., Miano, D., Bua, A., Alicai, T. and Fauquet, C.M. (2012).** The VIRCA project: Virus resistant cassava for Africa, *GM Crops and Food: Biotechnology in Agriculture and the Food Chain* 3(2): 93–103.
5. **Kung, Y.-J., You, B.-J., Raja, J.A.J., Chen, K.-C., Huang, C.-H., Bau, H.-J., Yang, C.-F., Huang, C.-H., Chang, C.-P., and Yeh, S.-D. (2015).** Nucleotide sequence-homology-independent breakdown of transgenic resistance by more virulent virus strains and a potential solution, *Scientific Reports* 5: 9804.
6. **DeRosier, C., Sulemana, I., James, H., Valdivia, C., Folk, W. and Smith, R. (2015).** A comparative analysis of media reporting of perceived risks and benefits of genetically modified crops and foods in Kenyan and international newspapers. *Public Understanding of Science* 24(5): 563–581.
7. **Valdivia, C. and Gilles, J.L. (2001).** Gender and resource management: Households and groups, strategies and transitions, *Agriculture and Human Values* 18(1): 5–9.
8. **Quisumbing, A.R. and Pandolfelli, L. (2010).** Promising approaches to address the needs of poor female farmers: Resources, constraints, and interventions, *World Development* 38(4): 581–592.

9. **Meinzen-Dick, R., Adato, M., Haddad, L. and Hazell, P. (2003).** Impacts of agricultural research on poverty: Findings of an integrated economic and social analysis, *EPTD Discussion Paper* No. 111. Environment and Production Technology Division, International Food Policy Research Institute, Washington, DC, USA.

10. **Ostrom, E. (2007).** A diagnostic approach for going beyond panaceas, *Proceedings of the National Academy of Science* 104(39): 15181–15187.

11. **Valdivia, C., Seth, A., Gilles, J.L., García, M., Jiménez, E., Cusicanqui, J., Navia, F. and Yucra, E. (2010).** Adapting to climate change in Andean ecosystems: Landscapes, capitals, and perceptions shaping rural livelihood strategies and linking knowledge systems, *Annals of the Association of American Geographers* 100(4): 818–834.

12. **Hayward, C., Simpson, L. and Wood, L. (2004).** Still left out in the cold: Problematizing participatory research and development, *Sociologia Ruralis* 44(1): 95–108.

13. **Valdivia, C., Danda, K., Sheikh, D., James Jr., H.S., Gathaara, V., Mbure, G., Murithi, F. and Folk, W. (2014).** Using translational research to enhance farmers' voice: A case study of the potential introduction of GM cassava in Kenya's coast, *Agriculture and Human Values* 31(4): 673–681.

Authors

Dr Harvey James, *Associate Professor of Agribusiness Management, University of Missouri, Columbia, USA*

Dr Corinne Valdivia, *Associate Professor in the Department of Agricultural Economics, University of Missouri, Columbia, USA*

Dr William R. Folk, *Professor of Biochemistry, University of Missouri, Columbia, USA*

Dr Dekha Sheikh, *Council Member, Multimedia University of Kenya, Nairobi, Kenya*

Dr Festus Murithi, Violet Gathaara, Milton Kengo, Charles Bett and Grace Mbure, *Kenya Agricultural and Livestock Research Organization (KALRO), Nairobi, Kenya*

Disease-resistant GM cassava in Uganda and Kenya during a pandemic

Nigel J. Taylor, Haruna A. Sekabira, Kenneth W. Sibiko, Anton Bua and John K. Lynam

The emerging pandemic of cassava brown streak disease (CBSD) presents a threat to cassava production in East Africa. Genetic modification (GM) of cassava for resistance to CBSD under field conditions was demonstrated in Uganda and Kenya between 2009 and 2012. The study described here was undertaken to determine if investment in GM cassava for delivery of CBSD-resistant varieties to smallholder farmers would be economically sound.

In 2014, smallholder cassava farmers and wholesalers in western Kenya and in northern, eastern and central Uganda were interviewed to evaluate their knowledge and acceptance of GM cassava. Interviewees were assessed for their awareness of the major constraints facing cassava production and their willingness to grow and sell GM varieties modified for resistance to CBSD. Information gathered was used to determine the potential adoption rates and economic benefits of deploying GM cassava to combat the rapidly increasing spread and impact of CBSD in East Africa. If deployed by 2025, the net benefit of the CBSD-resistant varieties is estimated at US$ 436 million in western Kenya and US$ 790 million in Uganda over a 35-year period. This indicates that the research

Research investment would be repaid many times over in the form of improved income and food security

76

investment would be repaid many times over in the form of improved income and food security for smallholder farmers in the region.

Originating from Latin America, the tuberous root crop cassava is now central to maintaining food security across much of tropical Africa. Cassava has been subject to a succession of pandemics, including cassava mealy bug and virulent forms of the two virus diseases, cassava mosaic disease (CMD) and CBSD. Indeed, virus diseases are presently estimated to cause annual losses of almost a third of the total crop.[1] CMD causes malformation of the leaves and reduced storage root yields, while CBSD induces serious necrosis of the edible roots, rendering the crop unfit for sale or consumption.

Over the last 15 years the incidence and severity of CBSD has increased, spreading beyond its traditional area of distribution in coastal East Africa to appear in Uganda and western Kenya. It is now spreading quickly through Central and Southern Africa to reach pandemic proportions. Delivery of robust, disease-resistant varieties to help cassava farmers secure their crop against the effects of CBSD is paramount but has proved to be difficult. Traditional breeding methods have been limited in their ability to tackle the disease due to lack of genetic resistance to the causal viruses in existing cassava varieties.

Engineering virus resistance

The Virus Resistant Cassava for Africa (VIRCA) project was initiated in 2006. Its objective is to improve smallholder livelihoods by delivering CMD- and CBSD-resistant cassava varieties to farmers in Uganda and Kenya.[2] VIRCA is

Traditional breeding methods have been limited in their ability to tackle CBSD due to lack of genetic resistance to the causal viruses in existing cassava varieties

77

Strategically targeted investment of public funds to benefit smallholder farming systems is essential if the desired social and economic returns are to be realised a collaborative public-sector project involving the Donald Danforth Plant Science Center (DDPSC), USA; the National Crop Resources Research Institute (NaCRRI), Uganda; the Kenyan Agricultural Livestock Research Organization (KALRO), Kenya; and the International Institute for Tropical Agriculture (IITA), Nigeria. VIRCA is employing GM technologies to develop cassava with robust resistance to both CMD and CBSD. The GM varieties are not expected to require high input levels of fertilisers or other agrochemicals and will fit into existing smallholder cassava farming systems in a manner identical to non-GM cassava. As a not-for-profit project, no premium cost for the technology will be passed to the farmer.

GM approaches to crop improvement have different objectives when applied by the public and private sectors. The private sector must operate within trait, commodity and market contexts that ensure profit at least to repay the investment in research, development and distribution costs. This often requires exclusive rights over the improved varieties, unless royalty-free rights are granted for humanitarian reasons. The public sector, in contrast, can deliver royalty-free planting materials to farmers, and focus on crops, traits and regions where no direct economic returns exist. The latter case is prevalent in Sub-Saharan Africa, especially for subsistence and semi-subsistence staple crops like cassava. Strategically targeted investment of public funds to benefit smallholder farming systems is essential, however, if the desired social and economic returns are to be realised. The present study was undertaken to evaluate if a GM approach can prove economically viable in smallholder agriculture in Africa. The virus-resistant GM cassava under development by the VIRCA project was used as a case study for this assessment.

Face-to-face evaluations were undertaken by interviewing approximately 450 cassava farmers and 60 wholesalers using structured questionnaires designed to determine their perceptions of the major constraints facing cassava production and marketing. Participants were also surveyed for their knowledge of biotechnology, to establish where they obtained such information, and whether this would influence their adoption of GM cassava varieties improved for resistance to CMD and CBSD. Data collected allowed statistical analysis for preference of different traits across a range of farm households and market conditions. This information was used to evaluate how such preferences would be met with the cassava varieties being targeted for genetic modification. It is rare for *ex-ante* impact studies – based on forecasts before the event rather than actual results – to include an *ex-ante* evaluation of adoption in this manner. This was achieved using a market research method termed conjoint analysis, which allows detailed assessment of the different valued attributes and traits within a crop product such as cassava. Variation in demand for these traits was assessed across households to determine which characteristics influenced demand for the GM varieties. The adoption potential was in turn used to determine the potential economic impact of deploying the virus-resistant GM cassava.

A number of critical decisions have to be made in the development and deployment of GM cassava varieties. Deciding which cultivars to genetically modify is critical. Smallholder farmers cultivate many different cassava varieties within the same agro-

Deciding which cultivars to genetically modify is critical

79

For relatively low-income farmers with limited education, a surprisingly high percentage indicated an awareness of biotechnology economic region, sometimes even within the same fields. Choice of cultivar for genetic modification has a number of dimensions, including adaptive range, cultivation and cropping characteristics, in addition to consumer traits such as cooking and eating qualities. These affect the ease and rate of adoption of cassava varieties, the geographic scale of uptake and, in turn, the potential economic benefits gained from deployment of a GM variety. The VIRCA project chose to modify two varieties – TME204 and Ebwanateraka – which have a history of cultivation by farmers in Uganda and western Kenya, and both of which possess consumption traits preferred by consumers. The initial trait focus was genetic modification for resistance to CBSD within cultivar TME204. TME204 possesses inherent resistance to CMD but is highly susceptible to CBSD. The present study of the potential impact of the VIRCA varieties comes midway through the development of the TME204 variety with GM resistance to CBSD, clearly demonstrated under regulated field trials in the two countries.

Principal findings

The survey of smallholder farmers and cassava retailers in 2014 highlighted differences between western Kenya and Uganda. In western Kenya farmers prefer fast-maturing CBSD- and CMD-resistant cassava varieties, whereas in Uganda farmers prefer high-yielding CBSD- and CMD-resistant varieties. The threat of virus disease was clearly recognised as a major concern among farmers in both countries, with CBSD tolerance being the most valued trait attribute in both locations. In western Kenya, a sweet taste and good flour significantly influence farmers when selecting a cultivar. A sweet taste is also preferred in Uganda, as well as short cooking time. These preferences are compatible with the trait attributes of the two varieties considered for genetic modification in the VIRCA project.

Both varieties were selected because they were popular among farmers before the CBSD pandemic. They both yield well (potentially more than 30 tonnes per hectare) and mature in a relatively short time (9–12 months). Both cultivars are recognised as excellent, with a sweet taste, soft texture and good flour quality. Analysis of the data collected from farmer surveys therefore confirmed the selection of these two cultivars as good targets for genetic modification with virus resistance.

For relatively low-income farmers with limited education, a surprisingly high percentage indicated an awareness of biotechnology. Approximately 50 per cent of the farmers surveyed in western Kenya and 58 per cent of farmers in Uganda responded as such. Importantly, this awareness of biotechnology resulted in over 90 per cent of farmers in both countries indicating willingness to grow the GM virus-resistant varieties, with the GM trait not negatively affecting the potential willingness of farmers to adopt them. In Kenya, farmer information on biotechnology was found to come primarily from other farmers, the Ministry of Agriculture and the Kenya Agricultural and Livestock Research Organization (KALRO). These government organisations would be expected to provide practical and accurate information on the GM varieties, especially as they would also be responsible for the initial multiplication and deployment processes. In Uganda, reliance is principally on other

The threat of virus disease was a major concern among farmers ... with CBSD tolerance being the most valued trait attribute

The need to manage information flow ... is an important outcome of this study farmers, radio or non-governmental organisations (NGOs) for information on biotechnology, though with NGOs there is some potential for confused or contradictory messages on this topic. The need to manage information flow in Uganda associated with the multiplication and deployment of the GM varieties is therefore an important outcome of this study.

Traders are often seen as gatekeepers for the potential acceptance of new and improved varieties, in effect anticipating consumer reaction. For cassava this is partly true given the large subsistence component of the crop, with on-farm consumption being the norm.

In western Kenya, about a third of wholesalers currently trade in the two cassava varieties (TME204 and Ebwanateraka) being targeted for GM virus resistance. The availability of these varieties was low when this study was performed. However, approximately 80 per cent of wholesalers responded that they would trade them if available. Some 70 per cent indicated that they would trade them as GM varieties and 80 per cent stated that they would sell them at a discounted price, with any discount expected to fall over time as consumers became more accustomed to the quality of the GM varieties.

In Uganda, there is little present market trade in the two varieties being targeted for GM disease resistance, at least in the larger wholesale markets for cassava. This is probably due to supply constraints resulting from the impact of CBSD, because traders knew of the varieties and responded that they would trade them if available. If the varieties were genetically modified, retailer responses indicated some reduction in the prospect of trading, but this was only about 10 per cent, with some increase in trading indicated if the GM varieties were to be sold at a 25 per cent discount. The strong implication generated by surveying wholesalers in both countries is that increased supplies of these varieties in the form of a GM product would be readily accepted by traders. Such increases in supply are expected as a result of the reliable yield gains generated by virus-resistant GM strains of TME204 and Ebwanateraka.

Benefits

The *ex-ante* analysis estimates of net benefits (i.e. net present value) for the release of the CBSD-resistant varieties are US$ 436 million in western Kenya and US$ 790 million in Uganda over a 35-year period, calculated using an adoption date in 2025. This produces an internal rate of return of around 50 per cent in both countries, a result comparable to rates of return found in other studies of agricultural biotechnology. For example, a recent meta-data analysis found that GM crops on average increased farmer yields by 22 per cent and farmer profits by 68 per cent.[3] In the present GM cassava study farmers are the principal beneficiaries, although consumer benefits are also significant. Such high rates of return can be expected when effective control measures are being deployed during a pandemic such as the current situation with CBSD.

For the GM cassava varieties studied here, the costs are therefore small in relation to the potential economic benefits. High adoption rates, large yield gains and relatively low research and development (R&D) investment costs are key aspects of the strategy being implemented by the VIRCA project. All these

Increased supplies of the target varieties in the form of a GM product would be readily accepted by traders

83

For the GM cassava varieties studied here, the costs are small in relation to the potential economic benefits

factors support the large economic return of GM cassava as determined in this study.

The potential impact of the GM varieties being targeted by VIRCA is characterised by the relatively small initial deployment area of western Kenya and Uganda. Even so, these results provide strong support for the strategy of deploying virus-resistant GM cassava varieties. They also provide support for the development of additional GM cassava varieties that meet farmers' preferred characteristics within the wider East, Central and Southern African regions. Such products would increase the impact of the technology and bring the benefits of CBSD- and CMD-resistant material to a greater number of farmers. Experience gained in Uganda and western Kenya should also reduce the cost of developing and testing additional varieties, further increasing the net benefits of the GM approach to CBSD resistance.

Conclusions

The potential of biotechnology, especially GM crops, is often exaggerated. However, trait deployment through genetic modification can play a strategic role in agricultural R&D in Sub-Saharan Africa. The development of virus-resistant GM cassava varieties is a good example of the strategic use of the technology, especially if combined with critical design options that optimise the potential adoption and economic impact of the GM varieties.

This study validates the approach being pursued by the VIRCA programme in terms of both the adoption potential of these varieties and the expected economic returns on the investments in the programme. The economic benefits, which average US$ 35 million a year across the two countries, are large, based on a number of factors and design decisions, including: (1) the choice of preferred varieties for genetic modification that will lead to high adoption within the target regions; (2) successful resistance to CBSD during an evolving pandemic; and (3) R&D costs that are low in comparison to the potential benefits. The *ex-ante* impact analysis supports the extension of this approach to other countries and sub-regions being affected by CBSD.

References

1. **Legg, J.P., Lava Kumar, P., Makeshkumar, T., Tripathi, L., Ferguson, M., Kanju, E., Ntawuruhunga, P. and Cuellar W. (2015).** Cassava virus diseases: biology, epidemiology, and management, *Advances in Virus Research* 91: 85–142.
2. **Taylor, N.J, Halsey, M., Gaitán-Solís, E., Anderson, P., Gichuki, S., Miano, D., Bua, A., Alicai, T. and Fauquet, C.M. (2012).** The VIRCA project: Virus resistant cassava for Africa, *GM Crops and Food: Biotechnology in Agriculture and the Food Chain* 3(2): 93–103. doi:10.4161/gmcr.19144
3. **Klümper, W. and Qaim, M. (2014).** A meta-analysis of the impacts of genetically modified crops. *PLoS ONE* 9(11): e111629. doi:10.1371/journal.pone.0111629

Authors

Dr Nigel J. Taylor, Senior Research Scientist and Principal Investigator, Donald Danforth Plant Science Center, St. Louis, USA
Haruna A. Sekabira, Research Associate and PhD Student, Department of Agricultural Economics and Rural Development, Georg-August-Universität Göttingen, Niedersachsen, Germany
Kenneth W. Sibiko, PhD Student, Department of Agricultural Economics and Rural Development, Georg-August-Universität Göttingen, Niedersachsen, Germany
Dr Anton Bua, National Crops Resources Research Institute, National Agricultural Research Organisation, Uganda
Dr John K. Lynam, Board Chair, World Agroforestry Centre, Nairobi, Kenya

The politics and economics of GM food production in China, India and Kenya

Carl E. Pray, Jikun Huang, Jun Yang, Ruifa Hu,
Latha Nagarajan, Bharat Ramaswami, Anwar Naseem,
Gal Hochman, and Sanjib Bhuyan

Two decades after the first genetically modified (GM) crops were commercially grown, their cultivation remains limited to a few crops in a few
countries. In India, China and Kenya no major GM food crops can be grown
legally. However, after many years of political paralysis on GM food production,
there are signs of change. China has laid out a pathway that starts with
industrial crops like cotton and then goes to indirect food crops such as corn
for animal feed, and finally to food crops.[1] The new Indian government has
allowed tests of GM feed and food crops including eggplant, maize and rice,
and suggested agricultural biotechnology as a possible area for foreign
investment.[2] Some key ministers and members of parliament in Kenya support
lifting the 2012 ban on GM food imports.[3]

Consumers as a group benefit from the lower food prices of GM food crops ... but rarely support GM crop policies

To understand the restrictions on GM food
production that have occurred despite the
scientific consensus that GM crops are safe for
human consumption and have considerable
societal benefits, our research examined the
economic, political and social forces that have
shaped biotechnology policies in China, India

and Kenya. The adoption of productivity-enhancing technologies like GM food crops has a direct impact on many groups, including input suppliers, farmers and the food and livestock industries, as well as consumers. If an interest group perceives that they can capture significant economic or social gains from the adoption of GM crops, they may lobby the government for policies to encourage GM adoption. Whether they succeed or not depends on how much political influence they have and whether their policy objectives diverge from those of their governments.

Consumer reaction

Research has shown that consumers as a group benefit from the lower prices of GM food crops, but despite these economic benefits they rarely support pro-GM crop policies. Our studies on the impacts of GM maize and rice in China, India and Kenya show that among the various stakeholders, consumers would be the major beneficiaries (Table 1). We did not, however, find any consumer groups that were actively supporting GM food in these countries.

Part of the reason for the lack of support is that while consumer benefits from GM crop production are large in aggregate, they are small at the individual level. We estimate that insect-resistant rice would cause a 2–4 per cent decline in rice prices in India and China and adoption of insect-resistant maize would cause nearly a 1 per cent decline in meat prices in China, while the adoption of insect-resistant and drought-tolerant maize in Kenya would also lead to a decline in consumer prices, albeit small.

The other reason for limited consumer support for GM food crops is concern about food safety.

While consumer benefits from GM crop production are large in aggregate, they are small at the individual level

Table 1. Distribution of benefits from the commercialisation of GM crops as a share of total benefits accruing as a result of their adoption

Country	China		India		Kenya
Methodology	General equilibrium model with international trade		Multimarket model		Economic surplus/partial equilibrium
GM crop	Bt rice	Bt maize	Bt rice	Bt maize	Bt and DT maize
Benefit distribution, %					
Seed and biotechnology firms	1.5	6.1	17	3	27
Pesticide industry	-1.2	0	id	id	0
Farmers	20.6	17.6	30	34	24
Processors	na	na	id	id	2
Feed and livestock industries	11.5	8.7	na	26	small
Food retailers	na	na	12	8	na
Consumers	67.6	67.6	42	29	47.9

Bt = containing insecticide-producing genes from the bacterium *Bacillus thuringiensis*
DT = drought tolerant na = not applicable id = insufficient data

Note: All models assume no government price support. In India, all these commodities except maize have price support. If the government is assumed to continue supporting farm prices of these grains, the total benefits to society would be the same, but many of the benefits to consumers shown here would go to farmers.

For example, in China in 2012, 45 per cent of urban consumers considered GM food to be unsafe, with just 13 per cent reporting it as safe and 42 per cent saying they did not know. Previously, from 2002 to 2010, the proportion of consumers that considered GM food unsafe was somewhat lower, at 13–18 per cent.[4] The increase in concern appears to be due to the negative media attention given to the preliminary approval of GM rice production in 2009, alongside a large number of unrelated food safety problems with milk and other food products that undermined consumers' faith in government food safety regulation.

Studies of urban consumers in India characterised them as somewhat concerned about the safety of GM food.[5] Research by our group further found that food safety was a major topic in the national newspapers that served urban consumers.[6] Surveys of Kenyan consumers during the period 2003–2009 found that most urban and rural consumers held positive views about GM food but that some urban consumers were concerned about food safety.[7]

Political lobbying by industry groups
Given that consumers are largely ambivalent towards GM crops, if not actually opposed to them, what other interest groups could champion or prevent their commercialisation? In many countries farmers played an important political role in promoting the commercialisation of GM crops – for example GM soybeans and maize in Brazil and GM maize in South Africa. Our studies, summarised in Table 1, show that farmers are the second largest beneficiaries of *Bt* maize and rice production after consumers, which is consistent with the results of previous studies.[8, 9] However, farmers played a very limited role in pushing for GM food crops in China, India and Kenya. The smallholder farmers of Asia and Africa are not well organised and have very limited political power to push technology policies, unlike the large commercial farmers of Brazil, Argentina and South Africa who produce for the export market.

Studies of urban consumers in India characterised them as somewhat concerned about the safety of GM food

Industry groups that could gain from GM food crops are better organised and more influential than farmers ... but have not been active in supporting GM crops

One important contribution of our study is to identify other significant interest groups that could gain or lose from GM maize and rice adoption: the biotechnology and seed industry, pesticide industry, feed and livestock industries, grain millers and exporters, and the food industry. Table 1 shows that some of these industries can increase their profits significantly, either because sales increase (seed and biotechnology firms) or their grain costs decline (the feed and livestock industries), but others lose money because their sales decline (the pesticide industry).

The industry groups that could gain from GM food crops are better organised and more influential than farmers. With the exception of the biotechnology industry, however, they have not been very active or effective in supporting GM food crop production for several reasons. First, foreign seed and biotechnology companies are perceived as a threat to the local seed industry and local agriculture by some groups. Seed firms in both Asia and Africa fear that they would lose their seed markets to multinational biotechnology companies. Second, until recently, the grain, feed and livestock industries have had sufficient supplies of grain from local production or imports, and have only latterly felt the need for GM crops in order to increase local production and lower their prices. Third, some important subgroups in these industries would lose money or would not benefit, so they work with anti-GM groups or remain silent in the debate. The pesticide industry loses sales and profits from the adoption of insect-resistant crops. Farmers who grow basmati and other fine rice varieties in India could lose export markets and profits if GM rice is commercialised but resisted by export destinations. For China, the food industry that exports rice-based products has already lost money because of extremely low levels of GM rice in their exports to Europe.

Successful lobbying depends on the goals and structure of national governments

The impact of the pro- and anti-GM coalitions on policy will depend on whether their goals are consistent with those of their governments. The governments of all three countries share the basic objectives of ensuring food security through low food prices while supporting the livelihoods of farmers. They differ, however, in their specific agricultural technology goals. China seeks to build a globally competitive agricultural biotechnology industry that is not dependent on imported food grain technology. In India, prior to the change of government in May 2014, the ruling coalition was split. One group wanted to encourage the development of GM crops by Indian biotechnology and seed companies while allowing foreign biotechnology firms to operate. Another faction wanted to stop the development of GM crops for ideological, food safety and environmental reasons. In Kenya, the science and agriculture ministries support the development of the local seed industry and royalty-free access to GM food technology through public-private partnerships. However, GM technology faced opposition within the government itself, with the Minister of Public Health pushing through the 2012 ban on GM imports.

The case of GM maize

The ongoing debate on whether to approve GM maize in these three countries shows how policies are shaped by economic interest groups,

Policies are shaped by economic interest groups, political lobbying and government objectives

The governments of all three countries share the basic objectives of ensuring food security through low food prices while supporting the livelihoods of farmers

political lobbying and government objectives.

In China, GM maize is likely to be commercialised in the next few years. Almost all China's maize is fed to animals or used by industry, and imported GM maize has been used for years as animal feed, so consumer objections are not expected to be serious. Meanwhile, the government and feed industry are concerned about their growing dependence on imports of American maize. Chinese scientists have developed their own insect-resistant and herbicide-tolerant maize traits, which are not patented by foreign companies. So commercialising GM maize could reduce dependence on foreign grain and be the beginning of a globally competitive agricultural biotechnology industry. In addition, cultivating GM maize would increase farm income and reduce farmers' exposure to insecticides.

In India it is less clear whether GM maize or other food crops will be approved. The new government has no major split in its agricultural technology objectives, and its goal is to increase foreign investment in general and specifically in agricultural biotechnology. However, there could be more opposition from consumers than in China since about 30 per cent of maize is consumed directly as bread rather than fed to cattle, and civil society is more opposed to GM food. Most maize farmers profit from growing GM cotton and would like to grow GM maize. Local seed industry support is mixed, since most seed industry benefits will go to the foreign seed and biotechnology firms that control the current maize seed market. Feed and livestock companies, meanwhile, are starting to be concerned about the availability of maize and have asked the government to allow GM maize imports.[10]

Whether the government in Kenya will approve GM maize in the near future is also unclear. Kenyan government agricultural scientists, foreign biotechnology firms and some foreign aid donors have been pushing for GM maize production and consumption. The seed industry, some large-scale farmers and the cereal millers provide limited political support for commercialisation. In Kenya, GM maize is likely to face more opposition from consumers than in China or India because it is the main food crop, and civil society organisations supported by foreign donors are very active in opposing GM food. With the new government of 2013, a new constitution and a completely new government structure, it is hard to know what will happen for GM maize in Kenya in the near future.

References

1. **China Daily (2015).** *China to Enhance Public Awareness of GM Technology.* Available at the Ministry of Agriculture website http://english.agri.gov.cn/news/dqnf/201502/t20150203_24951.htm (Accessed 24 March 2015).
2. **Suresh, N. and Chandan, S.R. (eds.) (2014).** Modi government likely to allow *Bt* brinjal, other GM crops soon, *BioSpectrum India.* http://www.biospectrumindia.com/biospecindia/news/219129/modi-government-allow-bt-brinjal-gm-crops-soon (Accessed 6 April 2015).
3. **ISAAA (2015).** Nairobi ABBC-2015 Declaration: Lift ban on GMO imports in Kenya, *Crop Biotech Update*, Special Edition, 16 April 2015. International Service for the Acquisition of Agri-biotech Applications. https://www.isaaa.org/kc/cropbiotechupdate/specialedition/2015abbc/default.asp
4. **Huang, J. and Peng, B. (2015** forthcoming**).** Consumers' perceptions on GM food safety in urban China, *The Journal of Integrative Agriculture.*

5. **Bansal, S., Chakravarty, S. and Ramaswami, B. (2013).** The informational and signaling impacts of labels: Experimental evidence from India on GM foods, *Environment and Development Economics* 18: 701–722.

6. **Ramaswami, B. (2014).** *Agricultural Biotechnology Debates in the Rural and Urban Press*, Symposium and Workshop on Genetically Modified Crops in Africa and Asia: Opportunities, Barriers and Constraints, 18–19 September 2014. Rutgers University, New Brunswick, NJ, USA.

7. **De Groote, H., Kimenju, S., Keter, F., Ngigi, O. and Gitonga, Z. (2014).** *But What do Rural Consumers in Africa Think About GM Food?* Symposium and Workshop on Genetically Modified Crops in Africa and Asia: Opportunities, Barriers and Constraints, 18–19 September 2014. Rutgers University, New Brunswick, NJ, USA.

8. **Brookes, G. and Barfoot, P. (2013).** The global income and production effects of genetically modified (GM) crops 1996–2011, *GM Crops and Food* 4: 74–83.

9. **Klümper, W. and Qaim, M. (2014).** A meta-analysis of the impacts of genetically modified crops, *PLoS ONE* 9(11): e111629.

10. **US Grains Council, New Delhi (2014).** Personal communication, May 2014.

Authors

Dr Carl E. Pray, Professor, Department of Agricultural, Food and Resource Economics, Rutgers, The State University of New Jersey, USA

Dr Jikun Huang, Director and Professor, Center for Chinese Agricultural Policy, Rutgers, Chinese Academy of Sciences, Beijing, China

Dr Jun Yang, Associate Professor, University for International Business and Economics, Beijing, China

Dr Ruifa Hu, Professor, Beijing Institute of Technology, China

Dr Latha Nagarajan, Research Economist, International Fertilizer Development Center, Washington, DC and Rutgers, The State University of New Jersey, USA

Dr Bharat Ramaswami, Professor, Indian Statistical Institute, New Delhi, India

Dr Anwar Naseem, Associate Research Professor, Rutgers, The State University of New Jersey, USA

Dr Gal Hochman, Associate Professor, Rutgers, The State University of New Jersey, USA

Dr Sanjib Bhuyan, Associate Professor, Rutgers, The State University of New Jersey, USA

Adoption and uptake pathways of biotech crops for small-scale farmers in China, India and the Philippines

Mariechel J. Navarro and Randy A. Hautea

F armers coax seeds to grow and thrive in order to feed, clothe and provide fuel for themselves, their families and the rest of humankind. For a
profession that builds on hope, the responsibility is great. Each day farmers
tend their farms with an optimism that the investment they make on their
land will eventually pay off in terms of higher yield, better productivity and
enhanced quality of life for their families and communities.

Biotech, or genetically modified (GM), crops have been offered as a modern
option for crop development to address the onslaught of pests and diseases,
the vagaries of weather and other challenges to growing crops. Contrary to
the notion that only farmers from developed countries are reaping the gains
of modern biotechnology, about 85 per
cent of farmers are small landholders in the *Small-scale farming in*
developing countries of China, India and *developing countries*
the Philippines.[1] *has been stereotyped*
as backbreaking,
The project on the Adoption and Uptake *unprofitable and*
Pathways of Biotech Crops by Small-Scale, *unappealing to*
Resource-Poor Asian Farmers: Comparative *the young*

95

Bt cotton production is still a male-dominated activity, but there is growing involvement of women in GM crop commercialisation in China

Studies in China, India and the Philippines was spearheaded by the International Service for the Acquisition of Agri-biotech Applications (ISAAA) to give a human dimension to the statistics on farmer adoption and uptake pathways of biotech crops and the changes these have brought about in the lives of resource-poor farmers. "Adoption" refers to how farmers acquire and eventually apply the knowledge and practices pertaining to the planting of a biotech crop, and "uptake pathway" involves the process of capturing how a biotech crop is introduced, adopted, spread and shared by farmers with others.[2]

Collaborators from the Center for Chinese Agricultural Policy, Chinese Academy of Sciences; the Indian Society of Cotton Improvement; and the College of Development Communication at the University of the Philippines Los Baños conducted three-country research in 2013 to gather insights on the following four questions:

1. Who are the biotech farmers?
2. What are the factors that farmers consider in adopting biotech crops?
3. How have they benefitted from adopting the technology?
4. Who influenced them in adopting biotech crops?

The research looked at Hebei, Shandong, Anhui and Henan provinces in the Huang-Huai-Hai cotton production zone in China, the cotton-growing states of Andhra Pradesh, Maharashtra and Punjab in India, and the maize-growing provinces of Pampanga, Iloilo and South Cotabato in the Philippines. These regions were surveyed to obtain farmer-related information. In addition, discussion groups took place in different communities of about 10-20 farmer respondents. A participatory rural appraisal method called Innovation Tree Analysis was used for the qualitative part of the study. The method enables researchers to determine how the adoption of a biotech crop has started and spread in specific communities. It distinguishes various types of adopters and identifies social, economic, political and cultural factors that influence adoption, contextualisation and spread of an innovation. Several of these exercises were undertaken in the different study areas to identify the patterns or uniqueness of adoption and uptake pathways in particular communities.

Who are the farmers using GM crops?
Traditionally, small-scale farming in developing countries has been stereotyped as backbreaking, not commensurate with the efforts exerted, unprofitable, and particularly unappealing to the young. But farmers planting biotech crops paint a different picture. While *Bt* (insect-resistant) cotton production is still a male-dominated activity, there is growing involvement of women in GM crop commercialisation in China. Based on focus group discussions, indications are that more and more women are attracted to the benefits of growing *Bt* cotton as there is less labour involved than would otherwise be needed for pesticide applications. The three country surveys showed the dominance of male farmers, but the increasing role of women in production was revealed in the focus group discussions.

In China, the latest study suggests feminisation in Chinese agricultural production. Field work in cotton production was mainly conducted by women because the men engaged in more of the off-farm

Limited access to information about the new technology and inadequate government support contribute to delayed adoption

97

It is not the government agricultural extension services that are crucial in farmer adoption of new technology ...

jobs. Evidence from the focus group discussions indicates that the reduction in pesticide use and the labour saved due to the adoption of *Bt* cotton benefited women.[3]

In India, women were particularly observed to take an active role in farm operations such as weeding, picking and crop cleaning.[4]

In the Philippines, 75.1 per cent of farmer respondents were male. Land preparation and marketing were their major responsibilities. Although the women's role was mostly in food preparation and budgeting, they were seen to be increasingly involved in managerial tasks such as funding farm activities, deciding on inputs and hiring labourers to work on the farm.[5]

Filipino men dominate the planting process but wives control the input costs and spending, and thus are major decision makers in the choice of crop to plant and the farming methods to adopt. In Indian households the planting of *Bt* cotton has become a family affair, with the household head taking on the more strenuous activities and the mothers and children helping to pick and clean the cotton bolls.

In India, it is a significant sign that *Bt* cotton is attracting the young, with more than 50 per cent in the 21–40 age bracket among those surveyed in the cotton-growing areas of Punjab, Andhra Pradesh and Maharasthra.[4]

Interestingly, in the Philippines even college graduates are venturing into GM maize production, thus finding it a viable income-generating option. For farmers in China, on average, the net revenue for *Bt* cotton from a unit of land is US$ 667.30 per hectare. In Anhui province, farmers earned US$ 860.30 per hectare, followed by farmers in Henan at US$ 657.40. Hebei farmers earned US$ 634.00 per hectare while

Farmer leaders or village cadres have become local champions of GM crops as they take frontline action in trying out the technology

Shandong farmers earned US$ 474.80 (2004 data).[3] The Philippines reports two to three times higher income from planting GM crops, while Indian farmers obtain twice the income compared to traditional varieties.[6]

Reasons for adopting GM crops

Higher economic and yield benefits, freedom from or reduced infestations of cotton bollworm or corn borer, and a dramatic reduction in pesticide use and frequency of spraying are the principal motivators for adopting GM cotton in the three countries. The presence of private traders who sell seeds and provide capital loans, as well as the trust and strong ties between the farmers that contributed to the information flow on biotech crops, also facilitated adoption.

Yet, as with any technology, there are certain factors that limit or delay the adoption and uptake of biotech crops (Table 1). These include lack of capital and the high cost of farm inputs, especially in India and the Philippines. The influence of elders and church groups skeptical of biotech crops in these two countries were also noted. In China, local seed companies could not meet the demand for biotech seeds in the initial years of commercialisation. Limited access to information about the new technology and inadequate government support also contributed to delayed adoption.

Table 1. Limiting factors in the adoption and uptake pathways of biotech crops

Category	Limiting factors
Economic	• Lack of capital (India, Philippines) • High cost of farm inputs (Philippines) • Inadequate supply of biotech seeds due to high demand in the initial release of the crop (China) • Poor availability of seeds (Philippines) • Low market price of harvests (Philippines
Political	• Indecisive local politicians (Philippines)
Cultural	• Influence of elders skeptical of biotech crops (India) • Influence of church groups who are against GM products (Philippines)
Agriculture-related	• Lack of land areas for biotech crop production (Philippines) • Unsuitability of farm area for biotech crops (Philippines) • Availability of alternative crops to plant (Philippines) • Unfavourable weather conditions (India and Philippines)
Communication-related	• Lack of knowledge of biotech crops (all countries) • Misinformation about biotech crops (all countries)

Interestingly, it is not the government agricultural extension services that are crucial in farmer adoption of new technology. Rather, farmer leaders or village cadres have become local champions of GM crops as they take frontline action in trying out the technology after seeing a demonstration field trial, sharing their knowledge and signalling commitment to spread the benefits to fellow farmers within and beyond their community.

Carlos Guevara, a Filipino early adopter of GM maize, was given the National Farmer of the Year Award and feted by the Department of Agriculture. A risk taker and innovator, Guevarra is an inspiration to farmers in his community who have tried the technology and reaped the benefits, thereby changing lives and communities. Filipino farmers planting *Bt* maize have registered unit yield increases of as much as 37 per cent, with a reduction in expenditure on insecticides of 60 per cent.[7]

Li Wenjing, a Chinese farmer from Hebei Province, was persuaded by his village council to grow *Bt* cotton. He tried planting the crop and noticed a significant reduction in the cotton bollworm population and use of pesticides compared to the traditional variety. As a result, his higher income enabled him to renovate his house and buy a new tractor and television set. Seeing the benefits and potential of the technology, Wenjing did not hesitate to recommend it to relatives and farmer friends in other villages.

Similarly, Mohammad Habibbudin, an Indian farmer from Andhra Pradesh, changed to *Bt* cotton after suffering a huge loss in yield due to bollworm infestation. This decision proved correct, as his eventual yield increased from some 1,000–1,250 kilograms per hectare using traditional varieties to around 2,500–3,000 kilograms per hectare using *Bt* varieties, and this was as a result of the control of the bollworm infestation rather than a direct increase in yield. Quite significantly, farmers in his village reduced the number of times they applied pesticides from 10–12 occasions on non-*Bt* cotton to only 2–3 occasions on *Bt* cotton for the control of other pests.[8]

Uptake pathways of GM crops

Field research indicates that early-adopting farmers in India and the Philippines take the risk of a new technology by trying out a

Early adopters are usually committed to sharing biotech crop know-how with their relatives and peers

It is not scientists, institutional advocates, extension officers or other government agents that play key roles in making farmers adopt a new technology

biotech crop which they initially heard about from a demonstration field trial set up by seed companies or from progressive village leaders. Other farmers in the community have a more "wait-and-see"' attitude, taking time to observe how things progress but becoming motivated to try the new crop after seeing the early adopters' convincing results of higher yields and bountiful harvests.

Early adopters are usually committed to sharing biotech crop know-how with their relatives and peers. Among the farmers and other actors in the farming system, knowledge-sharing is highly interpersonal and face-to-face. This is due to the strong prevailing peer system among farmers and the belief that they owe it to themselves and their fellow farmers to share what would benefit everyone in the community (Table 2).

In China, the role of village cadres is quite important in that they coordinate with technicians to arrange training and convince farmers to participate in activities. Hence, the factors that facilitate early adoption are three-fold: (1) support given by trusted village leaders for GM crop production; (2) close ties between farmers; and (3) avoidance of the heavy losses incurred by farmers cultivating non-GM crops.

Conclusion
The champions of GM crops are the farmers. It does not take much to realise that it is not scientists, institutional advocates, extension officers or other government agents that play key roles in making farmers adopt a new

Table 2. Facilitating factors in the adoption and uptake pathways of biotech crops

Category	Facilitating factors
Economic	• Financial benefits of cultivating biotech crops, e.g. good physiological and physical traits of crops, high quality and volume of harvests, lower expenses for labour and pesticides (all countries) • Proof of good yield and income provided by first and succeeding adopters (all countries) • Presence of private traders selling biotech crop seeds (all countries), providing capital loans for biotech crop production (India, Philippines), and buying harvests (all countries) • Availability of other financiers who provide the necessary capital for biotech crop production (Philippines) • Experience of financial losses from planting non-biotech crops in previous years (China, Philippines)
Political	• Village cadres help to coordinate *Bt* cotton training seminars and organise visits to *Bt* cotton demonstration fields (China) • Breeding contract between local seed companies and village chiefs for seed production (China) • Presence of farmer associations providing support, such as cooperatives (India, Philippines)
Cultural	• Trust and strong ties between farmers (all countries) • Rapid spread of information on biotech crops (all countries)
Agriculture-related	• Synchronised farming (Philippines) • Variety portfolio (China)

technology in the first place. At the end of the day, it is the individual farmer who makes the crucial decision of whether to plant a crop or not, decides on the variety to plant and adopts new techniques and cultural practices. He has tilled the land for so long, and has a wealth of experience informing what is best for him and his community.

Farmers are risk-averse and may need more progressive village leaders to outline the benefits of new technologies. Yet once they see the benefits there appears to be no turning back. Nevertheless problems still exist, requiring the participation and cooperation of both the public and private sectors.

The amazing fact is that farmer adoption of *Bt* cotton now accounts for more than 95 per cent of total cotton production in China and India, while 80 per cent of Filipino yellow corn farmers are planting biotech maize. Indeed, as an excerpt from the poem *The Farmer's Creed* articulates:

> *I believe that by my toil I am giving more to the world*
> *than I am taking from it, an honor that does not come to all men.*
> *I believe that my life will be measured ultimately by what I have*
> *done for my fellowman, and by this standard I fear no judgment.*[9]

References
1. **James C. (2013).** *Global Status of Commercialized Biotech/GM Crops: 2013.* ISAAA Brief No. 46. Ithaca, New York, NY, USA. Available at www.isaaa.org
2. **Navarro, M. and Hautea, R. (2014).** *Adoption and Uptake Pathways of GM/Biotech Crops by Small-Scale, Resource Poor Farmers in China, India, and the Philippines.* ISAAA Brief No. 48. Ithaca, New York, NY, USA. Available at www.isaaa.org
3. **Wang, X., Huang, J., Liu, H., Xiang, C. and Zhang, W. (2013).** *Adoption and Uptake Pathway of GM Technology by Chinese Smallholders: Evidence from* Bt *Cotton Production.* Center for Chinese Agricultural Policy, Chinese Academy of Sciences, Beijing, China. Available at www.isaaa.org
4. **Mayee, C.D. and Choudhary, B. (2013).** *Adoption and Uptake Pathways of* Bt *Cotton in India.* Indian Society for Cotton Improvement, Mumbai, India. Available at www.isaaa.org

5. Torres, C., Daya, R., Osalla, M.T. and Gopella, J. (2013). *Adoption and Uptake Pathways of GM/Biotech Crops by Small-Scale, Resource-Poor Filipino Farmers.* College of Development Communication, International Service for the Acquisition of Agri-biotech Applications SEAsiaCenter, and SEAMEO Southeast Asian Regional Center for Graduate Study and Research in Agriculture, Los Baños, Laguna, Philippines. Available at www.isaaa.org

6. ISAAA (2013). *Cadres of Change: Transforming Biotech Crops in China, India, and the Philippines.* International Service for the Acquisition of Agri-biotech Applications, Center for Chinese Agricultural Policy, Chinese Academy of Sciences; Indian Society for Cotton Improvement; and College of Development Communication, University of the Philippines Los Baños. Ithaca, New York, NY, USA. Available at www.isaaa.org

7. Yorobe, J. (2006). Economic impact of *Bt* corn in the Philippines. *The Philippine Agricultural Scientist* 89: 258–267.

8. ISAAA (2013). *Farmers First: Feedback from the Farm.* International Service for the Acquisition of Agri-biotech Applications SEAsiaCenter, Los Baños, Laguna, Philippines.

9. *The Farmer's Creed.* http:agricultureproud.com/2013/02/25/the-farmers-creed-poem-characteristics-of-a-farmer/

Authors

Dr Mariechel J. Navarro, Director of the Global Knowledge Center on Crop Biotechnology, International Service for the Acquisition of Agri-biotech Applications (ISAAA), Metro Manila, Philippines
Dr Randy A. Hautea, Global Coordinator, International Service for the Acquisition of Agri-biotech Applications (ISAAA), Metro Manila, Philippines

Honduras and *Bt*/HT maize – a small country model for GM crop adoption?

José Falck Zepeda, Patricia Zambrano,
Denisse McLean, Arie Sanders, Maria Mercedes Roca,
Cecilia Chi-Ham and Alan Bennett

To understand the role that genetically modified (GM) maize may offer in supporting increases in agricultural productivity and production in Honduras, the International Food Policy Research Institute (IFPRI), Zamorano University and University of California, Davis-PIPRA implemented a joint project examining the potential gains from adopting and using *Bt* (insect-resistant) and HT (herbicide-tolerant) maize in Honduras, and the institutional issues that help define impact. This chapter examines some key outcomes of the study.

Background to maize production in Honduras

Agriculture continues to be an important sector for the Honduras economy, with agriculture representing 13.4 per cent of total gross domestic product (GDP) in 2013.[1] Maize is the main staple crop and in 2012 generated 6 per cent of all gross crop production value.[2] With some fluctuation, maize production exhibited a steady increase during the 1960s–1990s, reaching a historic peak of 672,000 tonnes in 1995 (Figure 1). However, yields plummeted from 1.6 tonnes per hectare annually during

The Honduran government has expressed the need to increase maize production by reducing pest and disease damage through a wider use of technology ...

Figure 1. Maize production and yields, Honduras, 1961–2013

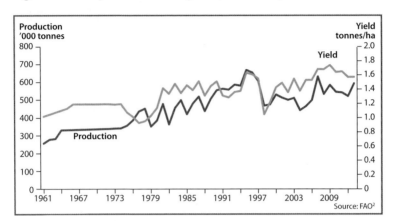

Source: FAO[2]

1995–1997 to little more than 1.0 tonne per hectare in 1998, a number that had not been seen since 1979. The sudden drop in both yield and overall production in 1998 reflected the devastating effects of hurricane Mitch, which negatively affected all sectors of the Honduras economy. It took several years to recover to pre-Mitch yield levels, and only in 2003 was the country able to reach yields similar to those registered in 1995. While yields have in fact recovered, production continues to be lower than in 1997.

Maize production is hampered by constraints including damage from pests and diseases, drought and climate change, and limited access to inputs as well as institutional and infrastructure issues.[3] Falling internal production has resulted in increasing dependence on maize imports to feed the growing population, for animal feed and industrial uses. While in 1961 Honduras imported less than 1 kilogram of maize per person, by 2011 this had grown to 62 kilograms, just below the amount it produced per person (Figure 2).

Figure 2. Maize production and imports, Honduras, 1961–2011

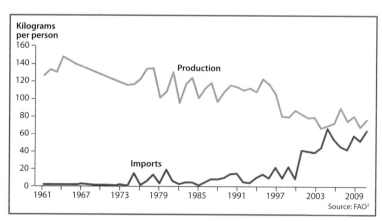

Source: FAO[2]

Given that maize is the main staple crop in the country, the increasing dependence on imports has created a food security concern for the government. For this reason Honduras has a strategic interest in aligning agricultural policies with major economic and trade partners but also needs to increase its own production and productivity.

A major constraint on increasing maize production in Honduras and Mesoamerica is the damage caused by lepidopteran insects, which is estimated to affect 40–70 per cent of total production.[4] Other relevant pests and diseases have increased as well, including fungal diseases along with the presence of mycotoxins.[5, 6, 7]

The Honduran government has expressed the need to significantly increase maize production by reducing pest and disease damage through a wider use of technology and by providing an enabling policy and regulatory environment that will help address the institutional constraints that dampen the country's maize production and productivity. The government has therefore initiated the implementation of an enabling set of policies that help facilitate the adoption of new technologies for maize and for the agriculture sector in general.

A systematic assessment of descriptive statistics shows that maize producers in Honduras have benefited from GM maize adoption

Enabling policies to support the adoption of modern biotechnologies implemented by the Honduran government include the establishment of a functional Biosafety Framework and Regulations in 1998, the establishment of a National Biosafety Committee in 2000, the incorporation of biotechnology into its National Food Self Sufficiency Strategy in 2008, and ensuring co-ordination and convergence towards a joint agricultural and environmental political agenda.[8] The establishment of these policies, in addition to the signature of free trade agreements and other international protocols regulating technology, genetic resources and varietal use, contributes to the overall goal of increasing the use of modern technologies such as hybrid and GM seeds as part of the formal Public Agricultural and Food Sector Strategy, which was set by the Ministry of Agriculture in 2012. These policy developments contributed to a functional biosafety system that was established in 2003 with the first commercial approvals for GM maize.

Adoption of GM maize in Honduras
Honduras started cultivating GM maize in 2002. By 2013, of the country's 400,000 hectares of maize, 29,000 hectares were planted to GM varieties.[9] The National Institute of Statistics in Honduras has estimated that approximately

Table 1. Producers sampled in Honduras, 2012

Type of producer	Plot size				Total	
	Less than 7 ha		More than 7 ha			
	No.	%	No.	%	No.	%
Non-adopters of GM	58	54	25	25	83	40
Adopters of GM	39	36	57	56	96	46
Partial adopters	11	10	19	19	30	14
All	108	100	101	100	209	100

75,000 hectares are cultivated with improved varieties – both conventional and GM hybrids – representing some 15 per cent of the total area planted.[10]

The GM hybrids planted in Honduras have insect-resistance and/or herbicide-tolerance traits. Strains approved for commercialisation with either single or stacked traits include the *Bt* strains MON810, Herculex® (Cry35Ab1 DAS-59122-7) and YGVTPro® (MON89034), as well as one glyphosate-tolerant strain, NK603.

Results from the first round of the survey and field studies conducted in a project funded by Canada's International Development Research Centre, implemented jointly by Zamorano University and IFPRI in 2008, showed that GM maize provided excellent target pest control in Honduras.[11] The *Bt*/HT maize yield advantage was 856–1,781 kilograms per hectare. Based on risk-adjusted estimations, the use of GM maize was preferred even by risk-averse producers. There was no significant evidence supporting overall pesticide reduction due to GM maize adoption, although there was significant statistical evidence that adopters achieved a higher net income than non-adopters in spite of GM seed costs being twice those of the conventional hybrids available in the market.

GM maize in Honduras: a descriptive analysis

In the IFPRI 2012 case study, a systematic assessment of descriptive statistics shows that maize producers in Honduras have benefited from GM maize adoption, at least for the producers sampled for this study (Table 1). In our sample, which was drawn from farmers who already used improved varieties (conventional or GM hybrid), adoption of GM maize was far less common among those with less than 7 hectares than for those with larger plots.

In line with the study done in 2008, the 2012 study shows that GM-adopting farmers tend to be commercial, progressive, and have more income as well as access to both credit and other productive inputs. However, the data collected fail to show the exact reasons why adoption has been mainly limited to commercial farmers, so a comparison between adopters and non-adopters in this study should not be used to extrapolate to a comparison between commercial and smallholder or subsistence farmers. In fact, adopters and non-adopters of GM maize in Honduras may be two distinct groups with unique characteristics that may be explained by variables unobserved in this study. Thus making a robust comparison between these two groups in terms of yield, net income and other metrics continues to be a challenge.

Table 2. The benefits of GM adoption in Honduras, 2012

Item	Plot type	Average	
		Raw	Adjusted
Yield (tonnes/ha)	a. GM	5.3	4.78–5.02
	b. Conventional	3.7	3.7
	c. Difference (a-b)	1.6	1.08–1.32
Income (US$/ha)	a. GM	1,774	1,584–1,754
	b. Conventional	1,244	1,244
	c. Difference (a-b)	530	340–510

More study is required to further elucidate the unique and specific characteristics of adopters and non-adopters, and to understand why smallholder or
subsistence farmers may not be adopting this technology.

An econometric analysis of GM maize use in Honduras
We performed advanced econometric procedure to deal with bias and outliers
in order to adjust estimates of the explanatory variables on yield and net
income. The adjusted results are more conservative than the averages estimated during the preparatory descriptive analysis. Results from the descriptive
analysis (Table 2) of the 2012 survey data show GM maize plots had on average
a yield advantage of 1.6 tonnes per hectare over conventional maize plots. In
turn, our econometric results, adjusted for statistical bias or outliers, indicate
a GM maize yield advantage of 1.08–1.32 tonnes per hectare. Statistical biases
and outliers were relevant in our sample, as using (raw) averages would overestimate the impact of GM maize on yields by 17–32 per cent.

In turn, as presented in Table 2, the descriptive analysis of the 2012 data showed
that there was a difference in income of US$ 530 per hectare between GM and
non-GM plots. As in the case of yield, adjusting these averages for statistical
bias or outliers results in a more conservative advantage of GM maize, ranging
from US$ 340 to US$ 510 per hectare. These
results are consistent with other assessments
done with *Bt* and/or HT maize elsewhere.[12]

*Farmers who
participated in our
study who had planted
only conventional
maize had little, if
any, knowledge of
GM maize*

**Small-scale farmers' perceptions and
attitudes and the maize value chain**
Results from qualitative assessments carried
out during our study, using small group

discussions and other qualitative techniques, gave interesting preliminary results in explaining small-scale farmer behaviour towards GM technology in Honduras. Our first-step assessment indicated that farmers who participated in our study who had planted only conventional maize had little, if any, knowledge of GM maize.

Qualitative assessments of seed distributors seem to indicate that it is not economically viable to reach dispersed small-scale and resource-poor farmers

Qualitative assessments of seed distributors seem to indicate that it is not economically viable to reach dispersed small-scale and resource-poor farmers. An important remaining question for future research would be whether small-scale farmers with accessible information and access to GM seeds would adopt the technology. The small sample of farmers in the qualitative analysis seems to support a positive response to this question.

A clear conclusion among the participants in small group discussions includes the importance of taste in determining the direction that maize varietal technology should take. There appears to be a significant connection between taste perceptions and preferences for varieties deemed traditional. A proper and systematic comparison between traditional improved varieties, hybrids and GM hybrids would be appropriate to further elucidate this difference. The results of our study appear to imply that taste preferences favour traditional varieties, while economic and agronomic factors favour GM maize.

We also conducted farmer consultations using structured group work. Results from this exercise need to be taken with some caution, as it was only possible to consult with a limited range of growers. The exercise appears to show that

113

Institutional issues such as lack of information, finance, credit and seed availability appear to limit adoption small-scale farmers in areas farther away from Olancho, the main commercial production area, seem to have weaker links with the rest of the actors in the value chain.

There appears to be a set of institutional issues such as lack of information, finance, credit and seed availability that limit adoption.

Churches were identified in the structured group work as one key actor in disseminating information and shaping perceptions. Thus any policy designed to increase availability of the new technologies and disseminate relevant information would benefit by taking this fact into consideration. Further explorations that consider the influence of food-use maize processors, feed mills and other industrial processors as well as small-scale producer associations will be warranted. It will be prudent for future work to consider the actual and potential role played by current seed distribution and conditional cash programmes regarding small-scale producers.

Initial consultations with food and feed processors show that there are differentiated market value chains for white and yellow maize. The major use of white maize is for human consumption whereas yellow maize is also used for animal feed and industrial purposes. Negotiated price agreements between government, producers and processors exist for both white and yellow maize.

The Central American Free Trade Agreement (CAFTA) is expected to enable the free import of yellow maize by 2016. However, increasing price volatility and dependence on imports have motivated animal feed processors to develop plans to increase local yellow maize production. This will help ensure less dependence on imports while opening up the potential for the expansion of domestic yellow maize production.

Summary and concluding reflections

The adoption and use of GM maize in Honduras has demonstrated positive economic benefits for adopters. The 2008 and 2012 studies show that GM maize reduces insect damage and in some cases increases yields by 29–35 per cent compared to the non-GM hybrid and conventional varieties. In both studies, production costs per hectare of GM maize were higher than for conventional hybrid and traditional varieties. However, with the reduction in damage and in some cases reduced pesticide application, the use of GM seed gives a positive net income for adopters. The higher cost of hybrid GM maize seed compared to conventional seed does not affect net income as seed costs represent a relatively small proportion of total production costs. This can nevertheless be a limiting factor for resource-poor farmers who have no access to credit or savings.

Multiple institutional and policy issues need to be addressed in order to answer a seemingly perplexing question, at least from a conventional economics point of view: why is the aggregate adoption rate in Honduras low and growing relatively slowly when the yield and financial return on the GM technology is so high? This discussion leads us quite prominently to constraints that are typical in the early

Studying the adoption of GM maize in Honduras has provided robust but limited evidence of the benefits of expanding the technology to other segments of the agriculture sector

Countries that want to promote GM and other biotechnologies need an enabling policy and regulatory environment

stages of the process, including a lack of adequate information and knowledge about modern maize varieties, which is a particularly important consideration for some farmers, farm size, liquidity or budget constraints and access to farm inputs.

We observed a growing issue of serious problems with pests and diseases beyond the target pest controlled by the GM maize. Black tar spot disease, caused by the pathogens *Phyllachora maydis* and *Monographella maydis* in association, affects conventional and GM maize alike. Farmers may be reticent to pay a premium for GM maize when they know that black tar spot disease is still likely to infect plants and damage production.

Seed companies may be constrained in their ability to deal with infrastructural and seed market issues given the geographical dispersion of small-scale producers. Indeed, Honduras is a small outlet for both GM and conventional hybrid maize, operating in a market where there are multiple maize processors linked to government programmes, with a differentiated (white and yellow) maize market and government/processor/producer pricing agreements tied to international prices. The latter opens the market to the potential impact of international price fluctuations and availability.

These studies have identified robust evidence that the adoption of GM and conventional new variety technology increases economic benefits. Understanding the limitations to further expansion is important to future research efforts to examine small-scale farmers' attitudes to GM technology adoption and potential impact.

Studying the adoption of GM maize in Honduras has provided robust but limited evidence of the benefits of expanding the technology to other segments of the agriculture sector. One clear lesson is that countries who want to promote the adoption and commercialisation of GM and other bio-technologies need to set in place an enabling policy and regulatory environment that supports technology research and development, transfer and adaptation to the specific country's needs. Honduras has a functional biosafety and regulatory system that may serve as a working example of an enabling environment that is eminently pragmatic in its implementation. We expect the lessons learned through this and previous studies to shed some light on the application of GM and other hybrid maize technologies, as well as other advanced innovations in other developing countries.

References
1. **WDI (2015).** *World Development Indicators*. Online database. http://databank.worldbank.org/data/views/variableselection/ selectvariables.aspx?source=world-development-indicators
2. **FAO (2015).** FAOSTAT. Online database. http://faostat.fao.org/
3. **Hintze, L.H., Renkow, M. and Sain, G. (2003).** Variety characteristics and maize adoption in Honduras, *Agricultural Economics* 29: 307–317. doi: 10.1111/j.1574-0862.2003.tb00167.x
4. **Hruska, A.J. and Gould, F. (1997).** Fall armyworm (Lepidoptera: Noctuidae) and *Diatrea lineolate* (Lepidoptera: Pyralidae): Impact of larval population level and temporal occurrence on maize yield in Nicaragua, *Journal of Economic Entomology* 90: 611–622.
5. **Resnick, S., Costarrica, M.L. and Pacin, A. (1995).** Mycotoxins in Latin America and the Caribbean, *Food Control* 6(1): 19–28.
6. **Bean, G.A. and Echandi, R. (1989).** Maize mycotoxins in Latin America, *Plant Disease* 73(7): 597–600.
7. **Rodrigues, I. and Naehrer, K. (2012).** A three-year survey on the worldwide occurrence of mycotoxins in feedstuffs and feed, *Toxins* 4(9): 663–675.

8. **Gomez, A. (2013).** *Honduras, Agricultural Biotechnology Annual 2013.* US Department of Agriculture (USDA), Washington, DC, USA.
9. **James. C. (2014).** *Global Status of Commercialized Biotech/GM Crops: 2014.* ISAAA Brief No.49. International Service for the Acquisition of Agri-biotech Applications. Ithaca, New York, NY, USA.
10. **INE Honduras (2013).** *Encuesta Agropecuaria Básica Mayo 2012.* Instituto Nacional de Estadística, Tegucigalpa, Honduras.
11. **Falck-Zepeda, J., Sanders, A., Rogelio Trabaniño, C. and Batallas-Huacon, R. (2012).** Caught between Scylla and Charybdis: Impact estimation issues from the early adoption of GM maize in Honduras, *AgBioForum*, 15(2): 138–151. http://www.agbioforum.org/v15n2/v15n2a03-falck-zepeda.htm
12. **Yorobe, J.M., and Smale, M. (2012).** Impacts of *Bt* maize on smallholder income in the Philippines, *AgBioForum* 15(2): 152–162. http://www.agbioforum.org/v15n2/v15n2a04-yorobe.htm

Authors

Dr José Falck Zepeda, Senior Research Fellow, International Food Policy Research Institute (IFPRI), Washington, DC, USA

Patricia Zambrano, Senior Research Analyst, International Food Policy Research Institute (IFPRI), Washington, DC, USA

Denisse McLean, Zamorano University, Honduras

Dr Arie Sanders, Zamorano University, Honduras

Dr Maria Mercedes Roca, Tecnológico de Monterrey (ITESM), Mexico

Dr Cecilia Chi-Ham (currently at HM Clause Inc.), while leading the Biotechnology Resources Program at the University of California, Davis-PIPRA

Dr Alan Bennett, Professor in the Department of Plant Sciences, University of California, Davis-PIPRA

Seeking sustainability for smallholders: *Bt* cotton in India

Glenn Davis Stone and Andrew Flachs

O f the various genetically modified (GM) crops in use today, none is planted by more smallholder farmers than *Bt* cotton. *Bt* crops contain insecticide-producing Cry genes from the bacterium *Bacillus thuringiensis*, expressing proteins deadly to many common cotton insect pests. Small-scale Indian cotton farmers in particular have struggled with pest management, and in 2013 over 90 per cent of Indian cotton farmers planted *Bt* cotton, more than in any other country. A pressing question in agriculture today is how sustainable the benefits of *Bt* cotton will be for these farmers.

Despite universal recognition of the importance of sustainability in agriculture, we often forget this aspect as we point to the short-term impact of GM crops. Sustainability is not simply a property of a technology, but a matter of how that technology is integrated into local agricultural practices. Extensive research has shown that sustainable smallholder farming is highly knowledge-intensive.[1]

Our research in India focused on the ways in which farmers develop local knowledge about crops and what this means for their sustainability. Research in Warangal District began before *Bt* cotton was released, with fieldwork in a set of villages representing

Sustainability is not simply a property of a technology but a matter of how that technology is integrated into local agricultural practices

119

farmers differing in caste, education and prosperity. Four villages were selected for long-term research on trends in cotton farming. We draw on this research to advance our knowledge of sustainability, first by examining patterns in cotton yields in the study villages (and also in the state and nation), and second by examining the long-term trends in seed choice that reflect how technology is or is not being integrated into local knowledge systems. In 2014 Warangal District became part of the new state of Telangana, but since our discussion covers a period when it was still part of Andhra Pradesh we use that name here.

Trends in cotton yields

The sustainability of *Bt* cotton cannot be understood separately from the recent history of the technologies used to grow cotton. Hybrid cotton seeds spread through India in the 1990s, marketed by rapidly proliferating and lightly regulated private seed companies, leading to a flood of seed brands.[2, 3] The hybrid seeds lacked resistance to Asian pests so uptake expanded along with heavy insecticide use. This technology package provided many farmers with quick profits and was rapidly adopted. But the insecticides lost effectiveness as pests developed resistance and beneficial insects were often killed off. During the 1990s and early 2000s, cotton farmers found themselves on a technology treadmill as they went through various types of insecticide, including organochlorines, organophosphates, carbamates, synthetic pyrethroids and spynosins. Seed brands appearing and disappearing from the market by the hundreds further challenged the stable integration of technology into local farm management.

During the 1990s and early 2000s, cotton farmers found themselves on a technology treadmill as they went through various types of insecticide

Figure 1. Cotton yields through time for India, Andhra Pradesh and the study villages, and *Bt* adoption as a share of India's cotton area

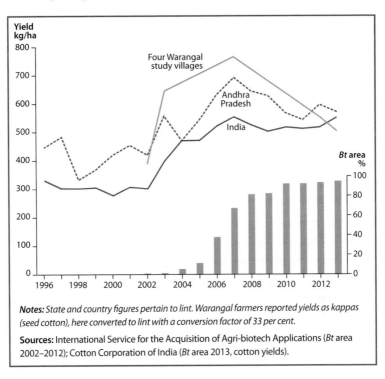

Notes: *State and country figures pertain to lint. Warangal farmers reported yields as kappas (seed cotton), here converted to lint with a conversion factor of 33 per cent.*

Sources: International Service for the Acquisition of Agri-biotech Applications (*Bt* area 2002–2012); Cotton Corporation of India (*Bt* area 2013, cotton yields).

Such practices were unsustainable; farmer debt rose to alarming levels, and many resorted to suicide.

Approved for sale in 2002, *Bt* cotton offered farmers a different insecticide technology. Cotton is plagued by both bollworms and sucking pests, two major categories of insect pests, and *Bt* genes produce proteins that are

Earlier studies tell us little about sustainability in a cotton sector with a history of unsustained benefits

lethal to bollworms. Initially, farmers in Andhra Pradesh – and in India generally – adopted *Bt* cotton slowly, but these numbers climbed rapidly during 2005–2007 (Figure 1). There have been more than a dozen studies attempting to isolate its impact on yields, most of which focused on the first few years after release, and most credited *Bt* seeds with significant yield increases[4, 5] as well as promising reductions in pesticide use.[6] However, these studies tell us little about sustainability in a cotton sector with a history of unsustained benefits.

A 2012 study estimated that, in sample villages in four states, *Bt* cotton increased yields by 4 per cent per year between 2002 and 2008.[7] And a further study that looked at our four Warangal villages over the period 2003–2007, during which time *Bt* cotton was widely adopted, found a similar average yield rise of 4.5 per cent per year.[3]

To consider yield sustainability, Figure 1 shows long-term yield trends for India as a whole, Andhra Pradesh and our four study villages in Warangal. In Andhra Pradesh, cotton yields had been rising at an average rate of 11 per cent annually for the three years before *Bt* cotton was first approved in 2002. In Warangal District, yields jumped by 66 per cent between 2002 and 2003, but this is apparently unrelated to *Bt* cotton as only 2 per cent of the sample farmers had adopted the new seeds. It was not until 2005–2007 that *Bt* adoptions surged, and since then yields have not risen. Since 2007, yields have stagnated nationally and fallen by 17 per cent in Andhra Pradesh. In our study villages, the decline has been yet sharper: yields have dropped to 34 per cent below the 2007 high.

Reasons for this decline are uncertain. An obvious concern is that, like previous generations of insecticides, *Bt* might lose its effectiveness, causing spraying to go back up and yields to go down. Krishna and Qaim's 2012 study concluded that the early pesticide reductions were sustainable,[8] but their data only went up to 2008 – the same year that *Bt* resistance was reported in one of India's worst bollworm outbreaks.[9] Still, to date there are no indications that *Bt* resistance has spread or that it is causing lowered yields.

However, India does have a problem with sucking pests that are not targeted by *Bt*. This problem has also been reported in China, where rising difficulties with sucking pests eroded the early benefits of *Bt* adoption.[10] In Warangal, farmers report particular problems with aphids, but recent studies show that mirids too have emerged as a key pest throughout much of India.[11] The role of *Bt* plants in driving this trend is debated. Exacerbating the problem is that most of the hybrids that *Bt* technology has been put into are large-boll cotton types that are more susceptible to sucking pests.[12] Overall, pesticide use remains lower than before the adoption of *Bt* cotton, but losses to sucking pests are a likely contributor to the slump in yields.[13]

Let us then turn to the larger question of how sustainably farmers have been able to develop local knowledge of the technology.

Integrating technology into farm management

Cotton farmers always have to deal with insects, but not all end up in a spiral of debt and suicide. We have noted the importance of local knowledge-intensive management in

Cotton farmers always have to deal with insects, but not all end up in a spiral of debt and suicide

With pest populations, seed brands and pesticides all changing very rapidly ... effective trialling of technologies was nearly impossible

sustainable farming; from this perspective the treadmill that Warangal farmers had been on was not an insect problem so much as a technology management problem. Earlier studies, before the introduction of *Bt* cotton, showed Warangal farmers having severe difficulties integrating new technologies into local agricultural practice. With pest populations, seed brands and pesticides all changing very rapidly, and with seeds and sprays inaccurately or deceptively labelled and marketed, effective trialling of technologies was nearly impossible. Instead of careful assessments, farmers turned to simple emulation of neighbours and followed the herd. Even before *Bt* became popular, the problem was reflected in short-term seed fads, in which one of the many seeds on the market would become wildly popular in a village for a few years. There was no clear agronomic reason for these fads, and farmers were unable to learn the properties of a seed before the next fad took over. Pesticide brands and technologies also changed rapidly, increasing the uncertainty in farmer decision making.[14]

The hope has been that *Bt* technology would provide more reliable insect control so that the new seeds would be more amenable to being sustainably integrated into local management practices. One concern in this regard is that *Bt* technology itself has changed rapidly: from one *Bt* technology (or transformation event) in 2002, there are now six different *Bt* technologies approved and more than 1,500 hybrids. K.R. Kranthi, head of the Central Institute for Cotton Research, sees the proliferation of seed brands as a primary cause of declining cotton yields. The huge number of approvals – more than 1,100 brands as of 2012 – makes judicious trialling of seeds nearly impossible,

Figure 2. Patterns in the cotton seed choices of farmers in the four Warangal study villages

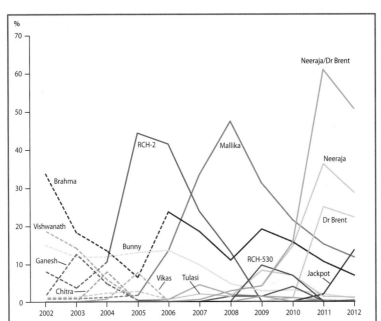

Random samples of farmers in each village were interviewed over the decade, reporting a total of 3,162 seed choices. The y axis shows what proportion of each year's seed choices were for the most popular seeds. Dashed lines before 2006 indicate conventional seeds; solid lines indicate *Bt* versions of the same seeds. Further details on the data and analysis are provided in Stone *et al.* (2014).

Note: Neeraja and Dr Brent are separate brands but they are almost identical. They are from the same company, released around the same time, contain the same Bollgard II event, were co-marketed in a new marketing strategy that is becoming more popular, and are often treated as interchangeable by local farmers.

> *It is when we look at the pattern of technology deployment that the appearance of unmitigated benefit begins to fade*

and also opens the door for unscrupulous marketing.[15]

Since we have found farmer technology assessment to be reflected in patterns of seed buying, we have analysed the history of seed choices spanning the period of Bt seed adoption. Figure 2 shows that the pattern of seed fads has not only continued but strengthened, with RCH-2 followed by Mallika, then Neeraja and Dr Brent. Continuing the pattern documented before, these seeds were not superior performers, as yields for Neeraja and Dr Brent were indistinguishable from those of other seeds. Their wild but ephemeral popularity was the result of a herd behaviour that develops when technologies are very difficult for farmers to assess.

Our long-term study of sustainability in cotton cultivation confirms the importance of looking at patterns in technology use rather than technologies in isolation. Taken in isolation, the hybrid seeds that spread in the 1990s should have been beneficial to the farmer, as test plots showed them to be higher-yielding than earlier varieties. Taken in isolation, each generation of insecticide should also have been beneficial to the farmer, as each showed initial effectiveness. And the Bt seeds adopted in the mid-2000s, taken in isolation, should have been beneficial as well, since they have shown effectiveness against one major category of pest. It is when we look at the pattern of technology deployment that the appearance of unmitigated benefit begins to fade. Simultaneous rapid change in seeds, pesticides and pests is destructive to the process of trialling that is essential in developing local knowledge of a technology and achieving sustainability.

India offers a sobering lesson for smallholder farmers seeking technological fixes to agricultural problems. Their focus must remain not only on sustained yield increases but on how technology is integrated into local agricultural practices.

References

1. **Netting, R.McC. (1993).** *Smallholders, Householders: Farm Families and the Ecology of Intensive, Sustainable Agriculture.* Stanford University Press, Redwood City, CA, USA.
2. **Lalitha, N., Ramaswami, B. and Viswanathan, P.K. (2009).** India's experience with *Bt* cotton: Case studies from Gujarat and Maharashtra, in: Tripp, R. (ed.) *Biotechnology and Agricultural Development: Transgenic Cotton, Rural Institutions and Resource-poor Farmers*, pp. 135–167. Routledge, New York, NY, USA.
3. **Stone, G.D. (2011).** Field versus farm in Warangal: *Bt* cotton, higher yields, and larger questions, *World Development* 39(3): 387–398.
4. **Qaim, M., Subramanian, A., Naik, G. and Zilberman, D. (2006).** Adoption of *Bt* cotton and impact variability: Insights from India, *Review of Agricultural Economics* 28(1): 48.
5. **Subramanian, A. and Qaim, M. (2010).** The impact of Bt cotton on poor households in rural India, *Journal of Development Studies* 46(2): 295–311.
6. **Kalamkar, S.S. (2013).** Biotechnology in Indian agriculture: Review of adoption and performance of *Bt* cotton, *Millennial Asia* 4(2): 211–236.
7. **Kathage, J. and Qaim, M. (2012).** Economic impacts and impact dynamics of *Bt* (*Bacillus thuringiensis*) cotton in India, *Proceedings of the National Academy of Sciences* 109(29): 11652–11656.
8. **Krishna, V.V. and Qaim, M. (2012).** *Bt* cotton and sustainability of pesticide reductions in India, *Agricultural Systems* 107: 47–55.
9. **Dhurua, S. and Gujar, G.T. (2011).** Field-evolved resistance to *Bt* toxin Cry1Ac in the pink bollworm, *Pectinophora gossypiella* (Saunders) (Lepidoptera: Gelechiidae), from India, *Pest Management Science* 67(8): 898–903.
10. **Wang, S., Just, D.R. and Pinstrup-Andersen, P. (2006).** Damage from secondary pests and the need for refuge in China, in: Just, R.E., Alston, J.M.

and Zilberman, D. (eds.), *Regulating Agricultural Biotechnology: Economics and Policy* pp. 625–637. Springer, Berlin, Germany.
11. **Udikeri, S.S., Kranthi, S., Kranthi, K.R., Patil, S.B. and Khadi, B.M. (2014).** Dimensions and Challenges of Altered Insect Pest Scenario under the Influence of *Bt* Cotton. Paper presented at the Sixth Meeting of the Asian Cotton Research and Development Network, 18–20 June, Dhaka, Bangladesh.
12. **Kranthi, K.R.** Personal communication.
13. **Peshin, R., Kranthi, K.R. and Sharma, R. (2014).** Pesticide use and experiences with integrated pest management programs and *Bt* cotton in India, in: Peshin, R. and Pimentel, D. (eds.), *Integrated Pest Management: Experiences with Implementation, Global Overview,* Vol. 4, pp. 269–306. Springer, Berlin, Germany.
14. **Stone, G.D. (2007).** Agricultural deskilling and the spread of genetically modified cotton in Warangal, *Current Anthropology* 48: 67–103.

Further reading

Qaim, M. and Zilberman, D. (2003). Yield effects of genetically modified crops in developing countries, *Science* 299: 900–902.
Stone, G.D. (2012). Constructing facts: *Bt* cotton narratives in India, *Economic and Political Weekly* 47(38): 62–70.
Stone, G.D., Flachs, A. and Diepenbrock, C. (2014). Rhythms of the herd: Long term dynamics in seed choice by Indian farmers, *Technology in Society* 36: 26–38.

Authors

Professor Glenn Davis Stone, Professor of Sociocultural Anthropology and Environmental Studies, Department of Anthropology, Washington University, St. Louis, USA
Andrew Flachs, Graduate Student of Sociocultural Anthropology, Department of Anthropology, Washington University, St. Louis, USA

Identifying and analysing barriers to the acceptance and use of GM rice

Eric Wailes, Alvaro Durand-Morat, Eddie Chavez,
Mohammad Alam, Francis Mwaijande, Hans De Steur,
Shoichi Ito, Zhihao Zheng, Alice Jin (Jiang),
Ranjit Mane and Francis Tsiboe

Rice is a major staple crop that feeds the world's people, accounting for 19 per cent of global food calories.[1] As the world's population grows, increasing numbers of people are in regions where rice dominates the diet, such as Asia, or where it is becoming more important, as is happening in Sub-Saharan Africa.

Genetically modified (GM) rice, unlike maize, soybeans, canola and cotton, is not yet produced or commercialised. But its promise includes nutritional and health benefits for poor households who suffer from childhood mortality, anaemia, blindness and other maladies that result from vitamin deficiencies in conventional non-GM varieties. Drought tolerance and plant-disease and insect resistance are also available from GM rice. Rice is water intensive and the introduction of drought tolerance would free up scarce water resources. Heavy use of herbicides, insecticides and fungicides can also be reduced through genetic modification, helping

As the world's population grows, increasing numbers of people are in regions where rice dominates their diet or is becoming more important

It is important to assess the awareness, responsiveness to information and choice of non-GM and GM rice among farmers and consumers

to improve the sustainability of the environment while reducing soil contamination and adverse toxic reactions among the farmers who apply these chemicals.

Our study on the barriers to acceptance of GM rice involved three broad areas of research: the policy and governance environment influencing agricultural choices, consumer and producer awareness and preferences, and issues of global production and trade.

The policy landscape of GM rice

Our exploration of the policy landscape of GM rice was made in nine countries and regions across the globe – Bangladesh, China, Colombia, the European Union, India, Japan, the Philippines, Tanzania and the USA – by scholars native to each country or region. Identifying the governance, approval process and status of GM regulation is important in understanding the way forward for GM rice commercialisation. In particular, the study questioned the decisions that seek to deny vulnerable populations and environments the choice of accessing the potential benefits that GM rice could provide, given available science-based information.

While addressing a similar set of issues across our study area, we found governance of the approval and commercialisation of GM products to be quite different from country to country. Issues included the relative importance of rice to the agricultural production and food consumption patterns of each country; the structure of the food and agricultural policy environment, the regulatory institutions for GM foods and the non-governmental organisations that represent producer, consumer and public interests; the development history of biotechnology and GM policy in each country; and the political, legal, regulatory and socio-economic barriers to the acceptance and use of GM rice. A critical assessment of these barriers in terms of the future likelihood of GM rice approval indicates that stark differences in the regulatory environment across countries pose major constraints and challenges to the harmonisation and commercialisation of GM rice in the global economy.

Consumer acceptance and producer adoption
It is important to assess the awareness, responsiveness to information and choice of non-GM and GM rice among farmers and consumers to better understand the constraints to commercialisation.

Our surveys of consumers and producers focused on several developing countries where rice is already an important food staple or becoming

Figure. 1 Consumer willingness to pay for GM rice: level of premium or discount considered acceptable by consumers

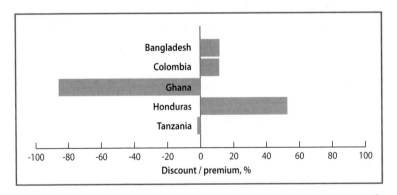

Figure 2. Producer willingness to adopt GM rice: share of farmers stating "definitely yes" to GM adoption if it confers a 10 per cent gain through improved yield, reduced cost or enhanced nutrition

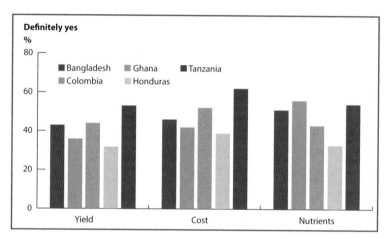

increasingly important. Awareness of biotechnology, objective and subjective knowledge about genetic modification, consumer willingness to pay and producer willingness to adopt GM rice were studied. Our consumer surveys were conducted in Bangladesh, Colombia, Ghana, Honduras and Tanzania in 2014. We find that consumer knowledge about GM technology is poor and awareness is very limited. Our studies introduced science-based information on the risks and benefits of GM rice traits for *Bt* (insect-resistant) rice and Golden Rice (rice genetically modified to biosynthesise beta-carotene, a precursor of Vitamin A). We tested the order in which the risk and benefit information was introduced as well as the type of GM trait. In general, we found very little difference between consumers across countries with regard to the order in which information had been imparted and the type of GM traits involved. However, as Figure 1 shows, there were wide differences across countries in consumers' willingness to pay a premium or their discount requirements in order to accept GM rice instead of non-GM rice.[2]

In our survey of farmers in Bangladesh, Colombia, Ghana, Honduras and Tanzania we assessed awareness and knowledge of GM technology and measured the probability that they would be willing to adopt GM rice for a given level of benefit either in yield improvement, reduction in costs of production, or improved nutrient health from rice for their family. Results on producer acceptance of GM rice show that incremental improvements in yield advantage, reduction in production costs and improvement in health benefits are positively related to GM rice adoption. Differences across countries vary in magnitude and by GM trait. Figure 2 shows survey responses. We depict the proportion of farmers who would definitely adopt GM rice if it conferred

Figure 3. Producer willingness to adopt GM rice: mean benefit required for producers to switch to GM rice from non-GM rice

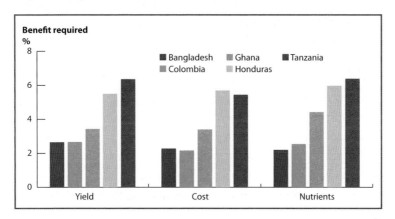

It is important to estimate the impacts of adoption in those countries best suited to adopt GM without disrupting international trade

a 10 per cent improvement in yield relative to non-GM rice, a 10 per cent reduction in production costs, or a 10 per cent improved nutrient health benefit for the farmer's family.

Figure 3 shows producers' willingness to adopt in terms of the level of benefit they would require for each of the three traits under consideration. Producers from Bangladesh and Colombia have the lowest benefit requirement threshold for switching to GM rice, while producers from Honduras and Tanzania have the largest. For instance, on average, producers from Bangladesh require a 2.6 per cent yield benefit to switch to GM rice while Tanzanian farmers require a 6.4 per cent yield benefit.

Global impact of *Bt* rice adoption

The final part of our study examined global production, trade and price impacts for a selected number of key rice-importing countries in a position to adopt GM rice to achieve greater self-sufficiency and food security. The commercialisation of maize, soybeans and cotton did not occur quickly. But as studies over the past 25 years have shown, adopting and commercialising these commodities has provided large economic, health and environmental benefits.[3,4,5] It is therefore important to estimate the impacts of adoption in those countries best suited to adopt GM rice without disrupting international trade.

To assess the impacts of GM rice commercialisation on the global rice market, we used the well-established Arkansas Global Rice Model (AGRM) and the RICEFLOW model to provide analyses of GM adoption.[6] Scenarios of adoption, diffusion and acceptance of *Bt* rice by Bangladesh, China, Indonesia, Nigeria and the Philippines were compared against baseline projections. The results focused on world trade, world and domestic prices, resource savings, domestic production, consumption and stocks. *Bt* rice adoption has the potential to significantly impact global and national rice economies. The total rice trade, international price and domestic prices decline as global rice production, consumption and stocks expand.

Given limited arable area for expansion, sustainability of production over the long run must come from productivity gains. The introduction of high-yielding rice varieties during the Green Revolution led to significant productivity increases and steady decreases in rice prices from 1975 to 2000. A new boost in rice productivity is urgently needed to cope with increasing demand and declining resources, and the "gene revolution" may be one of the many tools that can help achieve the intended goal.[7] Adoption of new seed technologies with higher productivity potentials, including GM rice, is one of several approaches for improving land productivity and water efficiency for rice cultivation. Yet rice and wheat, the two main food crops, are being held hostage by the controversy over GM technology.[3]

Concluding thoughts

The analyses conducted by this project provide a cross-sectional assessment of the constraints and challenges facing governments, consumers, producers, bioscience companies, and international organisations and foundations that are concerned about the future of food availability, food quality, environmental sustainability and the global rice economy. Research on this important topic must and will

Given limited arable area for expansion, sustainability of production must come from productivity gains

continue. Genetic improvements in a wide range of traits are necessary for one of the world's most basic staple foods. Acceptance and commercialisation of GM rice has benefits and risks. However, it is important to better understand the constraints and potential of GM rice in helping to meet future food demand, to help sustain the environment and to meet the health challenges of a very large population that depends heavily on rice as a basic food staple.

References
1. **FAO.** FAOSTAT online database. http://faostat.fao.org/
2. **Durand-Morat, A., Wailes, E., Alam, M.J., Mwaijande, F. and Tsiboe, F. (2015).** Multi-country Assessment of Barriers to Acceptance of GM Rice. Annual Meeting of the Southern Agricultural Economics Association, Atlanta, Georgia, USA. http://ageconsearch.umn.edu/handle/196980
3. **Demont, M. and Stein, A.J. (2013).** Global value of GM rice: a review of expected agronomic and consumer benefits. *New Biotechnology* 30: 426–436.
4. **Brookes, G. and Barfoot, P. (2013).** *GM Crops: Global Socio-economic and Environmental Impacts 1996-2011.* PG Economics Ltd, Dorchester, UK. http://www.europabio.org/sites/default/files/report/2013globalimpactstudy finalreport.pdf
5. **Klümper, W. and Qaim, M. (2014).** A meta-analysis of the impacts of genetically modified crops. *PLoS ONE* 9(11): e111629. doi:10.1371/journal. pone.0111629
6. **Durand-Morat, A., Chavez, E. and Wailes, E. (2015).** GM Rice Commercialization and its Impact on the Global Rice Economy. Annual Meeting of the Southern Agricultural Economics Association, Atlanta, Georgia, USA. http://ageconsearch.umn.edu/handle/196979
7. **Dawe, D. (2010).** *The Rice Crisis: Markets, Policies and Food Security.* FAO and Earthscan, London, UK.

Authors

Professor Eric Wailes, Distinguished Professor, University of Arkansas, Fayetteville, USA

Dr Alvaro Durand-Morat, Research Scientist of Agricultural Economics and Agribusiness, Department of Agricultural Economics and Agribusiness, University of Arkansas, Fayetteville, USA

Eddie Chavez, Senior Program Associate, Department of Agricultural Economics and Agribusiness, University of Arkansas, Fayetteville, USA

Dr Mohammad Alam, Associate Professor in Agribusiness and Marketing, Faculty of Agricultural Economics and Rural Sociology, Bangladesh Agricultural University, Mymensingh, Bangladesh

Dr Francis Mwaijande, Francis Mwaijande, Senior Lecturer of Public Policy and Social Science Research, Mzumbe University, Tanzania

Dr Hans De Steur, Department of Agricultural Economics, University of Gent, Belgium

Dr Shoichi Ito, Professor of Food and Agricultural Policies, Graduate School and Faculty of Agriculture, Kyushu University, Japan

Professor Zhihao Zheng, Professor in the College of Economics and Management, China Agricultural University, China

Alice Jin (Jiang), Department of Agricultural Economics and Agribusiness, University of Arkansas, Fayetteville, USA

Ranjit Mane, Program Associate, Department of Agricultural Economics and Agribusiness, University of Arkansas, Fayetteville, USA

Francis Tsiboe, Research Assistant, Department of Agricultural Economics and Agribusiness, University of Arkansas, Fayetteville, USA

Index

A

activism   15, 40
advocacy   38, 40
African Biosafety Network
    of Expertise (ABNE)   55
African Ministerial Conference
    on Science and Technology   54
agricultural policy   16, 33, 36, 39, 42,
        56, 57, 63, 87, 91, 108-109, 114,
        115, 117, 130-131, 134
agricultural research   7, 11–20, 23-26,
        36, 41-42, 47, 51, 76, 78,
Agricultural Research Council   14
agriculture sector   11, 109, 117
agrochemicals   78
anaemia   129
Andhra Pradesh, India   96, 98, 100,
        120-122
Angola   36, 39, 41
Anhui Province, China   96, 99
animal feed   63, 86, 92, 107, 114
anti-GM   25, 90, 91
aphids   123
approval/s   12, 21, 24-26, 36, 88,
        109, 124, 130, 131
Argentina   89
Arkansas Global Rice Model   134
Asia   89, 90, 95, 120, 129

B

Bacillus thuringiensis (BT)   25, 42, 44,
        49, 88, 89, 97-99, 101,103, 104,
        106-117, 119-127, 132, 134

banana   7, 14, 28-31
banana bacterial wilt (BBW)   28, 29,
        31
Bangladesh   130-135
barriers to acceptance   7, 130
barriers to adoption   14, 32
biodiversity   21
biofortified GM banana   31-33
biosafety   13-14, 16-17, 19, 25,
        40, 55-61, 109, 117
Biosafety Framework and
    Regulations, Honduras   109
bioscience   21, 135
biotechnology industry   88, 90, 91
black Sigatoka   28
Black tar spot disease   116
blindness   129
Botswana   39, 41
Brazil   21-26, 89
Breeding   29, 34, 39-40, 77, 103
Bt cotton   25, 44, 97-99, 101, 103,
        104, 119-127
Bt maize   88-89, 101,
Bt rice   88, 134-135
Burkina Faso   36, 39, 41, 42, 55, 56
Burundi   41

C

caloric intake   28, 129
Cameroon   36, 41
carbamates   120
carbohydrate   28, 30, 34
Cartagena Protocol on Biosafety   55
cassava   7, 12, 17-18, 62-74, 76-85

cassava brown streak disease
  (CBSD)   63, 76-85, 77-80, 84
cassava mealy bug   77
cassava mosaic disease
  (CMD)   63, 77-80, 84
Cedara   47
Census of Agriculture, Uganda 30
Center for Chinese Agricultural
  Policy   96
Center for Strategic and
  International Studies (CSIS) 11
Central Africa   77, 84
Central African Republic   41
Central American Free Trade
  Agreement (CAFTA)   114
Central Institute for Cotton
  Research   124
chemicals   19, 130
childhood mortality   129
China   7, 86-93, 95-104,
                     123, 130, 134
Church groups   99, 100, 114
climate   14, 21, 38, 54, 107
College of Development
  Communication, Philippines   96
Colombia   130-134
commercialisation   12-13, 15, 18-19,
           29, 36, 44, 62, 69, 72, 88, 89,
           93, 97, 99, 110, 117, 130, 131, 134
Common Market for East and
  Southern Africa (COMESA)   18
Community of Practice (CoP) 46-53
conjoint analysis   79
Consultative Group on International
  Agricultural Research institute
  (CGIAR)   38
consumer   14, 16, 19, 24, 29, 36, 48,
          56, 61, 64, 80, 82, 83, 87-89,
          92-93, 130, 131-133, 135

consumer preferences   16, 17, 67, 79,
                    80, 81, 113, 130
consumption patterns   65, 130
conventional hybrids   44, 49, 110, 115,
                              116
corn borer   99
Côte d'Ivoire   39, 41
cotton   12, 18, 22, 24-25, 42, 44,
          86, 92, 96-99, 101, 103-104,
              119-127, 129, 134
cotton bollworm   99, 101, 121-123
counterfeit products   16
cultivars   79-81

D

Dannhauser, South Africa   47
debt   121, 123
Democratic Republic of the
  Congo   39, 41
distribution costs   78
Donald Danforth Plant Science
  Center (DDPSC)   63, 78
drought tolerance   13, 63, 87, 88, 129
Durham University, UK   21

E

Early adopters   33, 100, 102
East Africa   11-20, 40, 56, 76-77,
                              84
East African Community (EAC) 18-19
East African highland banana   28
Ebwanateraka   80, 82-83
economic benefits   24, 51, 76, 80,
                    83-84, 87, 116
economics   86-93, 115
ecosystem services   21
education   16, 20, 31, 81, 120

eggplant 86
Estcourt, South Africa 47
Ethiopia 36, 39, 41
ethnicity 64
Europe 12, 15, 26, 91, 130
European Union 130
ex-ante analysis 79, 83, 85
exports 18, 19, 64, 89-91
extension 15-16, 18, 20, 31, 33-34, 47, 52, 69, 71, 85, 98, 100, 102

F

farmer associations 31, 33, 47, 49, 50, 51, 103, 114
fertilisers 51, 78
field trials 12, 13, 36, 80, 100, 102
Florianopolis, Brazil 24
food availability 135
food preparation 98
food quality 135
food safety 60, 87, 89, 91
food security 6, 11-12, 14, 17, 19-20, 21, 40, 43-44, 54, 58, 62-63, 65, 67-69, 72, 77, 91, 108, 134
foreign assistance 13
fungal diseases 108
Fusarium wilt 29

G

gender 31, 64-66, 71
gene revolution 135
gene silencing 65
Ghana 39, 41, 56, 131-133
global rice economy 135
globalisation 23, 25
glyphosate 23, 110

GM cotton 22, 24-25, 92, 99
GM foods, benefits 17, 19, 24, 46, 51, 54, 57, 61-63, 69, 71, 73, 76, 80, 83-84, 86-88, 92, 97, 99-101, 103, 111, 129, 130, 132, 134, 136
GM foods, risks 17, 43, 54, 57, 61, 62-74, 132, 136
GM hybrid 110, 111, 113, 115
GM technology 11, 13, 32, 44, 50, 91, 113, 116, 132, 133, 135
Golden Rice 132
governance 6, 15, 23, 26, 64, 130
Grain SA 47, 51
Green Revolution 135
gross domestic product (GDP) 6, 106
Guevara, Carlos 100

H

Habibbudin, Mohammad 101
health benefits 129, 133, 134
Hebei Province, China 96, 99, 101
Henan Province, China 96, 99
herbicide tolerance 49-51, 92, 106, 110, 129
herbicides 51, 129
Herculex® 110
high-yielding varieties 80, 135
Hlanganani, South Africa 47
Honduras 106-117, 131-134
Huang-Huai-Hai, China 96
human health 22
human resources 54, 59, 60
hurricane Mitch 107
hybrid 11, 37, 44, 46, 48-51, 106, 110-111, 113, 115-117, 120, 123-124, 126

I

Iloilo, Philippines 96
income 77, 92, 98-99, 101, 103,
110-111, 112, 115
India 21, 22, 24-25, 86-93, 95-104,
119-127, 130
Indian Farmers Association 53
Indian Society of Cotton
Improvement 96
Indonesia 134
industrial uses 86, 107, 114
information flow 82
Innovation Tree Analysis 97
inputs 49, 50, 72, 98-100, 107, 111, 116
insect resistance 42, 49, 87, 90, 92, 97,
106, 110, 129, 132
insecticide 88, 92, 119, 120-121, 123,
126, 129
intellectual property rights 17, 72
intercropping 72
International Development
Research Centre, Canada 110
International Food Policy Research
Institute (IFPRI) 106, 110-111
International Institute for Tropical
Agriculture (IITA) 78
International Service for the
Acquisition of Agri-biotech
Applications (ISAAA) 96
investment 13, 15, 20, 34, 77-78, 84,
86, 92, 95
Itithini, Kenya 70

JK

Japan 130
John Templeton Foundation 6, 21
Katumani, Kenya 67

Kenya 11-14, 17, 19, 36, 40, 41, 56,
62-74, 76-85, 86-93
Kenya Agricultural and Livestock
Research Organization
(KALRO) 62, 63, 67, 70, 71, 78, 81
Kranthi, K.R. 124
Kwanalu 46, 47, 49, 51, 53
KwaZulu-Natal (KZN) 46, 47, 49, 51
KZN University 50

L

LaMarque, Sandy 51
labour 46, 50, 97, 98, 103
Latin America 77
lepidopteran insects 108
Lesotho 36
Li Wenjing 101
Liberia 39, 41
Lima 47, 51
livestock industry 64, 81, 87, 88, 90,
93
lobbying 89, 91-92

M

Machakos, Kenya 67
Madagascar 36, 39, 41
Maharashtra, India 96
maize 12, 18, 22-23, 24-25, 46-51,
70, 86-93, 96, 98, 100-101, 104,
106-117, 129, 134
Malawi 36, 40, 41
Mali 39, 41
Mallika 125-126
market/s 16, 18, 31, 34, 40, 47, 51,
64, 65, 67-78, 70-73, 78-79,
82, 89-90, 92, 98, 100, 110,
114, 116, 120, 124, 134

matooke   28-33
Mbuvo, Kenya   70, 71
media   7, 11, 19, 40, 44, 58, 60, 64,
                                   65, 67, 88
Mesoamerica   108
Mexico   21-22, 24-25
milk   89
Minister of Public Health and
    Sanitation, Kenya   12
Ministry of Agriculture,
    Honduras   109
Ministry of Agriculture,
    Kenya   70, 71, 81
mirids   123
MON810   110
Monographella maydis   116
Monsanto   47
Mozambique   36, 39, 41, 56
Mtwapa, Kenya   67
mycotoxins   108

N

Nairobi   67, 69
Natal Agricultural Union   53
National African Farmers Union   53
National Agricultural Research
    Organization (NARO), Uganda   29
National Agricultural Research
    System (NARS)   38
National Biosafety Committee,
    Honduras   109
National Crop Resources Research
    Institute (NaCRRI), Uganda   78
National Food Self Sufficiency
    Strategy, Honduras   109
National Institute of Statistics,
    Honduras   109
Neeraja and Dr Brent   125, 126

nematodes   28
New Partnership for Africa's
    Development (NEPAD)   55, 61
Niger   39, 41
Nigeria   36, 39, 41, 56, 78, 134
NK603   110
no-till   49
non-GM hybrid   115
non-governmental organisation
    (NGO)   11, 15, 17, 36, 38, 39, 42, 46,
             47, 50, 56, 64, 68, 82, 130
North American Free Trade
    Agreement (NAFTA)   25
nutrients   73, 132-134
nutritional content   72

OPQ

Olancho, Honduras   114
open pollinated   48, 49, 50
organochlorines   120
organophosphates   120
Pampanga, Philippines   96
pandemic   76-85
Pannar   47
papaya ringspot virus   65
participatory research   65-66
peer system   102
pests and diseases   14, 19, 29, 95, 107,
                                   108, 116
Philippines   95-104, 130, 135
Phyllachora maydis   116
Pietermaritzburg, South Africa   48
planting materials   32, 78
policy makers   15-17, 19, 33, 44, 54,
                                   56, 61, 69
political debate   44
politicians   12, 57-59, 100
politics   13, 86-93

poor   32-34, 49, 66, 72, 96, 113,
                    115, 129
population   6, 21, 33, 54, 107, 130,
                    136
preferences   16, 17, 29, 64, 67, 73,
                    79, 113, 130
private sector   40, 44, 64, 78, 104
processing   38, 64, 67, 68, 71
productivity   11, 14, 37, 42, 72, 87, 95,
                    106, 108, 135
profits   13, 78, 83, 90, 120
protest movements   22, 25
Public Agricultural and Food
   Sector Strategy, Honduras   109
public funds   78
public opinion   44
public-private partnerships   91
public sector   44, 64, 78
Punjab, India   96, 98
qualitative assessment   31, 56, 97,
                    112-113
quantitative exercises   31

R

RCH-2   126
regulatory frameworks   23, 36, 40
regulatory system   12, 14, 16, 17, 24,
                    26, 54-61, 117
religious bodies   57
research and development (R&D)   38,
                    41, 83, 84, 85, 117,
resistance   29, 32, 49, 64-65, 73, 76-85,
                    110, 120, 123, 129
responsible innovation   26
rice   86-91, 129-137
RICEFLOW model   134
risk assessment   22, 57, 59
Rwanda   39, 41

S

sales   90
sampling   31, 56
science, technology and innovation
   (STI)   58-59
scientific capacity   12, 14, 17
scientists   16, 19, 22-23, 25, 32, 56, 62,
                    67-70, 72, 92, 93, 102
seed breeders   16
seed companies   36, 38-40, 42, 47, 91,
                    99, 102, 103, 116, 120
seed distribution   16, 50, 114
seed fads   124, 126
seed industry   37, 90-93
seed production   39, 103
seed sector   36-45
Senegal   39, 41
Shandong, China   96, 99
Sierra Leone   39, 41
soil contamination 130
soil fertility   47, 49
soil testing   51
Somalia   39
sorghum   7, 12
South Cotabato, Philippines   96
South Sudan   39, 41
Southern Africa   40, 56, 77, 84
soya/soybeans   22-24, 89, 129, 134
spynosins   120
stakeholder   26, 32, 44, 48, 50, 52-53,
                    56, 61, 62, 64, 65-69, 72-74, 87
staple   14, 18, 28, 30, 34, 39, 78, 106,
                    108, 129, 131, 136
storage   34, 47, 51, 77
Sub-Saharan Africa   16, 37, 38, 40, 56,
                    63, 78, 84, 129
subsistence   46, 78, 82, 111
sucking pests   121, 123,

sustainability 21-27, 119-127, 135
Swaziland 36
sweet potatoes 17
synthetic pyrethroids 120

T

Tanzania 11-20, 36, 39, 41, 130, 131-134
technology transfer 47, 117
Telangana, India 120
TME204 80, 82-83
tobacco 44
trade 18-19, 82-83, 88, 99, 103, 108, 109, 130, 134-135
traditional practices 23, 72, 77, 97
traditional varieties 46, 99, 101, 113, 115
trainers and educators 18, 47
training 47, 49, 59, 102, 103
transparency 23, 24, 60
trends 11, 15, 120, 122
trialling 124, 126

UV

Uganda 11-20, 28-35, 40, 41, 56, 76-85
Ugandan Science Foundation for Livelihoods and Development 18
UK 7, 26
University of California, Davis-PIPRA, USA 106
University of KZN, South Africa 47, 50
University of Missouri, USA 47, 48, 49, 62
University of Pretoria, South Africa 52

uptake pathway 95-104
urban public 23, 24, 65, 88-89
USA 7, 12, 63, 78, 130
value chain 37, 112, 114
village cadre 100, 102, 103
viral resistance 64, 65, 73
Virus Resistant Cassava for Africa (VIRCA) 78-85
Vitamin A 29, 32, 132
vitamin deficiencies 129
vulnerability 65, 67, 69

WXYZ

Warangal District, India 119-126
water 19, 58, 129, 135
Water Efficient Maize for Africa (WEMA) 13
weed control 23, 46, 49, 50-52, 98
weevils 28
wheat 135
wild races 29
willingness to adopt 132, 133
willingness to pay 36, 131, 132, 133
women in farming 62, 66-68, 70-73, 97-98
YGVTPro® 110
yield 28, 30, 72, 77, 81, 83, 95, 99, 101-103, 106-107, 110-112, 115, 120-124, 126-127, 132-134
Zambia 36, 40, 41
Zamorano University, Honduras 106, 110
Zimbabwe 36, 40, 41